Collecting
Moorcroft Pottery

Francis Joseph
ISBN 1870703-537

© Francis Joseph Publications and Robert Prescott-Walker 2002

Published in the UK by
Francis Joseph Publications, 5 Southbrook Mews, London SE12 8LG

Typeset by
E J Folkard Print Services, 199 Station Road, Crayford, Kent DA1 3QF

Printed in Singapore

ISBN 1-870703-53-7

Contents

Acknowledgements

I am deeply grateful to Walter Moorcroft, as well as his wife Lis, and to John Moorcroft and his wife Gill, all of whom I have known for several years. They have generously tolerated me dropping round, all too infrequently, for a chat, and not to mention the odd whiskey or two. As a consequence of this commission, I was extremely grateful to both families for allowing me to formally interview them over three or four days with specific questions. I also asked for their assistance in proof reading the chronology of their family and of the significant events of the pottery, along with a list of the patterns produced by the Moorcroft pottery. I am very grateful for the numerous amendments, comments and observations that they made to these listings. I am also very appreciative of the words of wisdom and insight over the years, from my early Sotheby's Chester days to the present, gleaned from specialist Moorcroft dealers John Donovan and Angela Stones of Rumours, London.

I am particularly grateful to Rebecca Wintgens, Grant Deudney and Elizabeth Hastings and Sarah Kirkham of Sotheby's, London, to Sharon Ashbolt of Sotheby's Sussex and to Christina Prescott-Walker, Sotheby's, New York Ceramics department for all the generous amount of time and trouble taken to locate and supply almost all of the colour illustrations, transparencies and digital, along with prices, etc.

I am also very grateful for additional images from Joanna Friedland of Phillips, De Pury, Luxembourg, London and to Gorringes Auction Galleries, Lewes, for the image of the pair of carp vases.

A special thanks goes to the library staff at the Hanley reference library, Bethesda Street, for all their efforts between 1979 and 1998 in locating and transporting all those volumes I used during my various research projects. As a consequence I have been able to produce numerous articles and now this book which is the sixth so far.

I am also very grateful to a band of highly skilled workers who were around in the early 1990s, namely the workers, 'Moorcroft girls', technicians, works manager, shop manager, salesmen, in fact everyone involved in the daily life of the Moorcroft Pottery from directors to part-time shop assistants and, of course, senior designer Rachel Bishop.

Introduction

"Founded in 1913 and still in production as an independent pottery today." This is something that can only be said of a handful of potteries in Stoke-on-Trent. That the initial design concepts and creative process responsible for the wares conceived in the late 1890s by William Moorcroft, are still very much alive and largely unaltered to this day is something almost certainly unique to Moorcroft amongst the Potteries.

Initially, the basic concepts behind what was to become synonymous with the Moorcroft Pottery, the use of slip as part of the surface decoration, were established by Mr. Wildig and continued by Richard Lunn during the early 1890s, at the firm of James Macitnyre & Co. The use of this technique was furthered by Harry Barnard, art director from 1895, but it was left to William Moorcroft, Harry Barnard's replacement in 1897, to realise the full potential of the technique. William not only mastered and further developed the technique into what it is today but was quick to realise the lyricism and full blown fluidity of the technique in terms of design, in the marriage of shape and surface pattern, and later added to this the subtleties possible in the skills of the paintresses, especially the potential of shading in all of its guises.

As a consequence of the merits of his designs which had gained high praise both nationally and internationally, winning several awards and gaining the plaudits of influential retailers such as Tiffany's of New York and Liberty's of London, not to mention Royal praise, William felt confident enough to open his own enterprise. With the financial backing of Liberty's William was able to set up his own new factory, the most modern model pottery with it's attention to all the latest innovations and thoughts regarding safety, improved working conditions and efficient production flow all on the ground floor. This partnership lasted until 1960 when Walter bought out Liberty's shares and therefore their financial and directorial involvement (not that there had ever been a great deal of the latter) the Moorcroft Pottery became solely owned for the first time by the Moorcroft family. In recent years with the rekindled interest in contemporary Moorcroft, largely on the back of the keen collectors and dealers interest in either the old or early Moorcroft designs, Liberty's has once again become involved with the sale of Moorcroft pottery and indeed has commissioned not only exclusive pottery designs but also ties and scarves with Moorcroft designs.

Everything involved with the production of the wares at the Moorcroft pottery, from the raw materials, the making of the shapes, the designs, decorating, firing, selecting and selling of the wares has to form a cohesive and balanced structure. What should not be forgotten is that at Moorcroft one man was responsible for the creation of every design, both shape and pattern, working with the thrower and main decorators. That same man was also responsible for the daily running of the business, promotion, advertising, sales and exhibitions. Stretched in all directions the weaker of the disciplines is certain to show signs of strain, especially as demands are extended in other areas and potential problems are glossed over or put back to be resolved at some later date. William fell into this trap of complacency amidst the heady success and demand of the early years, rewarded with major international awards, which gleaned ever more prestigious critical acclaim, yet, the business accounting and practice side of things was not running very well. With order books filled to capacity and production in full flow everything appeared to be running smoothly and a great success. An independent production manager brought into the works in the 1930s or even earlier would certainly have been aware of some potential problems of accountability in relation to the costs per piece produced.

As popular as Moorcroft is today it is hard to believe that the firm ever had lean years and at one time almost ceased to exist. As with many High Street products and household names the setters of 'fashion' or 'trends' often have strong followings and little sympathy for those items not encompassed within 'their' criteria. Moorcroft Pottery undoubtedly found it difficult in certain decades, especially from the 1960s through to the 1980s. Full order books to the point where meeting demand and orders was proving difficult and the general outward appearance of a health and vigorous company can be deceptive. Rising production costs and inefficiencies of flow-through of products can be neglected or over-looked in the flurry of filling orders and creating new designs. The furthest thing from the mind when such activity is going on can be the cumulative effect of economic conditions, closure of significant orders and rising costs of wages and materials, some of which are to a large part beyond normal control and yet have damaging effects.

John Moorcroft discovered, shortly after he joined the firm, that the staple and longest running product of the pottery, Powder Blue, was actually losing Moorcroft a great deal of money due to the increased cost of materials over the years and the man hours involved. This was something that only came about because John had the time to devote to working out the actual costs.

William Moorcroft examining a pot. (October 1923).

To fully understand the significance and importance of the wares produced at the Macintyre and Moorcroft potteries under the name of Moorcroft, the reasons why such ware was made and influences behind it need to be examined and understood. To do this one also needs to appreciate something about the competition and contemporaries in the pottery industry throughout this period as well as something of the contemporary political and social scene that surrounds the period, all of which inevitably had a bearing on output, style and pricing levels, etc. The 'lean' period, in terms of Moorcroft sales, of the 1950s and 1960s is a case in point with the new 'contemporary design' scene so much in evidence. The numerous coal strikes and union action, not to mention the financial collapse, during the 1920s also obviously took its toll. Moorcroft did not escape unscathed and it is interesting to examine how it had to adapt and react to such external events.

The history of the Moorcroft pottery as with so many other successful factories is one of balance. The expectation of a certain standard, the delivery of well thought out and balanced designs, the thorough training and pursuance of a high level of skill in the execution of the design and production and the recognition that the client should expect delivery at the appointed time are all part of the mix. In more recent times the exclusivity and the general hype of the 'limited edition collectables' market along with clever marketing strategy and available only on the day items for members of the collectors club and/or pieces only available at certain limited Moorcroft events throughout the year has seen a blurring of the delivery times. It is now part of the exclusivity that one has to wait at least a year or more for certain items to be delivered.

The current resurgence of interest in Moorcroft both old and new is perhaps indicative of a general international interest and indeed a revival in things floral and colourful, reflecting home furnishing trends. The turn of the twenty-first century has naturally spawned numerous commemorative and reflective exhibitions, articles, books, etc, related to artists of the Arts & Crafts movement, Art Nouveau. 1997 was a huge celebration for followers and devotees of Moorcroft as it was the centenary year. The Moorcroft management put on lavish displays for members, were involved with two exhibitions, etc. A good time was had by all and rightly so. How many other firms can boast such longevity, that has been for most of it's life run by the same family and still has family members on the board having given years of service to the family firm that is now run by newcomers, albeit some of the most ardent fans of Moorcroft and its history.

Technique

If there is anything that makes Moorcroft pottery different from its competitors, it is the techniques involved in its manufacture. Of these techniques the use of tube-lining is the most obvious and most readily associated with the name. Subtler, but no less significant however, is the method of painting as well as the colour palettes used and over the years the ingredients of the body, certain glaze effects such as the flambé effects. The body was also unusual in the early years as William choose to use or rather continued to use, following his days at Macintyre & Co, a very refined clay capable of withstanding very high firing temperatures, more usually used to make electric insulation-type wares and wares for chemical and pharmaceutical use. Over the years the body has changed little but due to alterations in the grinding and processing of the raw materials the body has undoubtedly changed. The high firing nature of the body, the way the limited range of colours fuse with the body in the initial firing, traditionally called the biscuit firing, is all part of what makes Moorcroft pottery what it is.

It should be realised that 'slip-trailing' as a technique has a long history in British ceramic production. It had been used with great skill and dexterity by several other firms in the latter part of the nineteenth century, most notably at the Doulton Lambeth works. There Henry Doulton produced numerous commemorative wares with 'white piped', as they called it, outlining as well as numerous inscriptions.

At this time the firms using the 'white piped' or 'slip trailed' technique were using as a vessel a stoneware ink pot, some 2½" high, with a small hole drilled towards the base at the side. A quill was fixed into the hole allowing the watered down clay or slip to escape from the inkwell. Once the inkwell was filled with slip and held in the hand, the

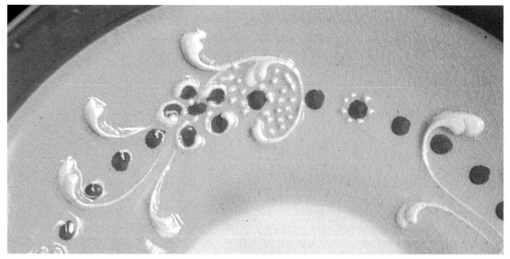

Detail of a Gesso Faience saucer by Harry Barnard, 1890s, showing the early use of slip trailing with very short staccato lines with very thin tails. The very watery use of the slip trailing enabling two sometimes three heads or starting blobs to be used in a decorative way. The watery thin slip also enabled tiny dots to be completed.

quill protruding forwards between the middle fingers, the flow was controlled by covering or uncovering the aperture of the inkwell with the thumb. The rate of flow of the slip was largely dependent on the consistency of the mixture which would have to be thin enough to flow freely from the vessel or inkpot with gravity as its only propellant. To a lesser extent the rate of flow would also be dependent on the angle at which the vessel was held in relation to the item being decorated. There are other factors that make the rate of flow variable such as the temperature of the slip and the rate of drying, amongst others. For instance, after the slip trailers had held the inkwell in their hands for any length of time the heat from their hands would affect the drying rate of the slip as the temperature of the inkwell increased. The temperature of the room and seasonal temperature variations would all have an effect on the slip, although perhaps to only a very small degree.

One of the biggest technical problems using the inkwell method of application of slip was that the inkwell had to be kept upright, more or less, severely limiting the radial movements or freedom of movement of the slip trailers. The vessel was more likely to be the object that moved. The inkwell method largely restricted the design possibilities to short, staccato lines or decorative motifs such as small dots, circles, etc.

The significant development that enabled this decorative technique to realise its full potential was almost certainly developed by William Moorcroft. William must have

been very aware of the limitations of the technique he inherited from Harry Barnard, no doubt brought on by his frustration at the inability of the slip trailers to carry out his new designs. Due to lack of records both in the factory archive and in the family this 'frustration' is purely conjecture but is based on accounts of others in the pottery industry, and how solutions to similar problems occurred in the industry. By studying the problems inherent in the restrictive inkwell technique William, who wanted to produce designs with long flowing lines of elongated leaves, plant stems, etc, must have realised that only through constant pressure of slip could the slip be forced into a consistent long line. The solution to this problem was to apply hand pressure to a bag containing slip with the line of slip formed by a quill or a similar device. It is this new device or method of applying long lines of slip that is best described by the term 'tube-lining', implying a strong degree of control and dexterity. The term 'slip-trailing' should therefore be applied to the old method of decoration, that still

Detail of a Aurelian ware jug, 1890s, printed and enamel painted with gilt slip trailing used to outline the pattern and for further detailing

Detail of a Florian ware vase by William Moorcroft showing the early use of his much longer and thicker slip trailing. There are some breaks in the lines indicating both the lack of control and perhaps a thicker than necessary use of slip.

favoured by country and studio potters, which include the application of slip with a brush or stick, to trail the slip onto the surface to create a design. The 'white-piping' method of applying slip for inscriptions or to outline designs through the use of gravity via an inkwell-style vessel being used in the 1860s was a precursor of the tube-lining method which seems to have been developed in the late 1890s.

In the early twentieth century Harry Barnard was credited with the 'invention' of the 'tube-lining' technique, indeed there are even contemporary reports that credit the technique to Harry Barnard along with an unpublished journal by Harry Barnard that has by some been seen to back up such contemporary suggestions. However, reviewing the evidence one finds that Harry Barnard was supported and written up as the inventor of the technique by his great friend Frederick Rhead. Also that Barnard's unpublished journal, written in 1931 many years later, seems to refer to a different aspect of the decorative techniques that he used, some of which appear to have already been devised by Mr Wildig and/or Mr Richard Lunn prior to Harry Barnards arrival at Macintyre & Co.

It was Frederick Rhead who gladly took over the girls that Harry Barnard had trained up at Wedgwood in his method of slip decoration which he had continued after he left Macintyre & Co. An examination of the wares produced for only a few years at Wedgwood by Barnard, before his designs were withdrawn, reveal that they were much the same as those he produced at Macintyre & Co with a mixed use of stencilling, deep incised markings, multi-layering of slip and short staccato piped lines of slip. It should also be acknowledged that Frederick Rhead was an influential figure and acknowledged commentator on design and methods of decoration in the pottery

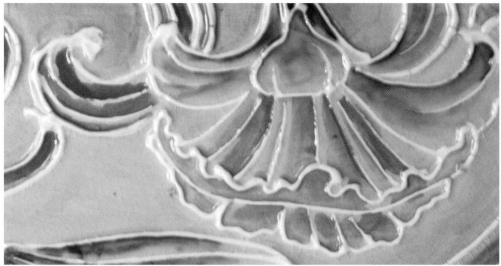

A detail of a Florian ware plate by William Moorcroft again showing the early use of slip trailing as a pattern outlining device to separate different colours and at the same time create an area that can hold complex shading techniques. The slip has become thinner and shows a greater degree of control.

industry during this period, making a major contribution to the development and achievements of the industry.

The unpublished journal, written so many years after the events and during the height of William Moorcroft's success, states that "I took up my position at Messrs Jas. Macintyre's at Cobridge – Washington Works – early in February 1895. It was one that I made for myself to introduce a new type of design, and a process which I had invented. As a name for it was required I called it 'Gesso' as it was a pâte-sur-pâte modelling and the tool to produce it was one that I had made. This proved to be quite a surprise – nothing quite like it had been done before." He carries on, "To make it a commercial line I introduced also an appliqué of 'slip' in a form of stencil pattern and the slip modelling was a free hand treatment that covered up the spaces necessary in the stencil pattern and so hid to a great extent the fact that it was applied in that way." The important words here in relation to the slip-trailed part of this whole process being that "the slip modelling was a free hand treatment that covered up the spaces necessary in the stencil....." This can only refer to the short staccato lines of slip that can be seen on the various examples of Barnards wares, these lines often being formed of three over lapping of conjoined lines that make up a fleur-de-lis like style motif.

The journal was seemingly written by a bitter man who had not gained the 'artistic' recognition he would have wanted or felt he deserved. Indeed, there is no doubt that Barnard was a skilful designer but perhaps his designs did not generate enough interest or praise to make them economically viable which resulted in him parting company with Macintyre in favour of Wedgwood. Barnard had a very good career with Wedgwood on the retail and promotional side of the business where he was a highly regarded figure and held an important position. He became particularly knowledgeable about Wedgwood as a company and its history. However, his feelings of being unjustly treated at Macintyre & Co which all but brought to end his designing career can only have been heightened following his replacement by William Moorcroft who within three years of his appointment was gaining significant praise for his new designs. When William quickly went on to become an internationally recognised pottery designer winning awards at most of the major international fairs in Europe and America followed by opening his own pottery with the support of Liberty & Co, gaining even greater success, Barnard must have felt acutely wronged. It was always William Moorcroft who was the focus of attention for the numerous articles, awards and praise, rather than the firm he worked for James Macintyre and Sons.

Following such a successful use of the tube-lining technique is wasn't long before numerous other potteries, especially those in the tile businesses, saw the possibilities of a method of decoration that so aptly reflected the contemporary style of the decade namely Art Nouveau. In many respects it was some of these wares that can be said to have used the art and skills of tube-lining at their most expressive, especially the Successionist range of wares produced at the Minton works as well as some superb tile designs, individual tiles and panel designs, by various tile manufacturers. The designs at Moorcroft pottery have a far closer relationship to the ideas and examples proposed by William Morris by reflecting nature in all its glory.

It was left to the extraordinary skills of the paintresses to fullfill the task of capturing essence of nature and hold it under a glaze. Although, historically this method of surface decorating has a very long a varied tradition in relation to the decorating of ceramics, there were certain skills developed by the Moorcroft paintresses, (I use the term paintresses advisedly as until recent years this position was almost always

Detail of a William Moorcroft Fish vase showing the use of slip trailing as a decorative end in itself showing details of the fish scales and fins with the colouring used to enhance the solidity of the fish. By now the tube-liners have complete mastery of the technique and it's subtleties through the use of the rubber bag containing the slip and the glass pipette.

occupied by women), that become equally as synonymous, if more subtly so, with the name of Moorcroft. Multi-layering of colours on top of one another, sometimes using four or five layers to achieve a desired effect was a skill developed after years of training and it was both time consuming and costly. Once a ground colour was washed into a certain area it might then need to be rubbed out to a certain degree to form a shaded area. Another method of creating a shaded area or graduated shading was to float a colour on the surface by a tube-lined edge and then with a damp brush quickly draw out some of the paint while it was still wet on the pot, the paint being drawn back up onto the damp brush. The then left a graduated dark pooled colour by the tube-lined wall gradually fading to a pale area where the brush was held. Quite frankly, some of these skills have to be seen to be truly understood and admired

The overall number of colours used in one design, the amount of layering required, the rubbing back of a base colours and the drawing out of colours all added to the time it took to complete a piece, making those pieces with complex requirements more expensive. Designs were, and still are, deliberately introduced that required a minimum of painting time and/or tube-lining time in an effort to have a regular flow of work for all concerned. Finding a correct balance between such designs so that all the tube-liners and all the paintresses are continually employed, the mould makers are making sufficient ware, balanced with profitability, popularity of wares, fulfilling orders, etc, etc, was and remains an immensely difficult task and one that perhaps was only sufficiently realised or at least undertaken whole heartedly in recent years.

Moorcroft Chronology

1869   Thomas Moorcroft (born 1849) and Theresa Edge (born 1849), both aged 20, married 27 March.

1872   William Moorcroft born in Riley Street, Burslem, second son of four to survive childhood.

1879   Harold Moorcroft, the youngest brother born

1880   Eleanor Francis Moorcroft died 3 October aged 4.

1881   Theresa Moorcroft died, aged 32.

1884   Betsy Jones, having been brought in to look after the boys became their stepmother.

1885   Thomas Moorcroft died in January.

1894   Macintyre show new art wares at the Exhibition of Decorative And Artistic Pottery, London. These wares, 'Taluf' and 'Washington Faience', were designed by Mr Richard Lunn and Mr Wildig.

1895   Harry Barnard joins Macintyre in February, having previously worked at the Doulton Lambeth Studio as assistant to Mark V. Marshall.

1897   William Moorcroft appointed designer at Macintyre's. The date William began work appears to be 22 March at the age of 24.

1898   New designs registered – Aurelian being one.

William Moorcroft promoted to Manager of the Ornamental Ware. Florian Ware introduced and within a year it was selling in Liberty's of London, Tiffany's in New York and Rouard of Paris. It was also bought in bulk by G. J. Bassett of New York.

1904   William Moorcroft won the Gold Medal at the St Louis International Exhibition. It is worth mentioning that is was William that won the medal and not Macintyre's. The factory was for the moment content to bask in the reflected glory as William set about making both a National and an international reputation for himself.

1910   William Moorcroft awarded a gold medal at the Brussels Exhibition.

1911   Harold Moorcroft emigrated to America.

1912	William Moorcroft told that his department at Macintyre's was to close on 30 June, 1913, in a letter dated 21 November.
1913	William Moorcroft was awarded the Diploma of Honour at Ghent, Brussels.
	After long and protracted negotiations William finally purchased a suitable site for a new purpose built modern factory, and came to an agreement with Macintyre's to transfer all or many of his former department employees, paintresses and decorators as well as important technical workers. The financial side was agreed between Liberty & Co. and William, Alwyn Lasenby Liberty and William being the two directors with Liberty having the controlling interest having put up two thirds of the monies. By the end of August William and his new team, approximately 34 people, were able to move into the new building. More negotiations were required with his former employers to purchase his shape moulds.
	William Moorcroft married Florence Lovibond, 30 April. Later moving into their new House in Trentham, 'Glendair'.
1914	Beatrice Moorcroft was born, 28 July.
1915	British Industries Fair – the company's first trade fair, and one which went on to become an important annual event up to 1939. Queen Mary visiting the Moorcroft stand every year.
1917	Walter Moorcroft born on 12 February.
1919	War Memorials Exhibition at the Victoria and Albert Museum.
	Special flambé kiln built.
1924	British Empire Exhibition held at Wembley. Edward Maufe designed the Moorcroft stand.
1925	Exposition des Arts Decoratifs in Paris
1926	Florence Moorcroft died in June of pneumonia.
1928	William Moorcroft received the Royal Warrant, 28 March. Later the phrase 'Potter to Her Majesty the Queen' was used as an impressed backstamp and/or on an applied paper label as well being used in advertisements and such like.
	4 October William and Hazel Lasenby (a relation of the owner of Liberty's) married at St George's, Hanover Square, London.
1930	William Moorcroft won the Grand Prix award at the Antwerp International Exhibition.

1933   William Moorcroft won a diploma of honour at the Milan Fair.

1935   Walter started work at the pottery having just finished school.

             British Art in Industry Exhibition at the Royal Academy.

1937   Walter Moorcroft designed a powder bowl with a lily flower which was bought at the British Industries Fair by the Duchess of Gloucester.

1938   William John S. Moorcroft born 29 March.

1945   William Moorcroft suffered a severe stroke in September. Walter Moorcroft, whilst serving in the army, having received a telegram hurried back to England on compassionate leave arriving on 30 September. Two weeks later on the 14 October William died.

             Walter Moorcroft assumed control of the pottery.

1946   Royal Warrant transferred to Walter in March. This expired in 1978, twenty-five years after the death of Queen Mary.

             Walter met and later married Molly Blakely on 7 December. Moving into Easedale on 12 February 1947.

1947   Special unmanned British Industries Fair, although Walter was asked to be on his stand when Queen Mary visited.

1948   Jean Moorcroft was born 3 November.

1950   Walter Moorcroft introduces a single moulded octagonal ashtray into production with great success. Decorated with an open Columbine.

1951   Festival of Britain – Moorcroft Blue or Blue Porcelain tablewares were chosen to be exhibited along with some other wares.

             Sheila Moorcroft was born 19 April.

1953   British Industries Fair. Last one to be held before the development of the International Spring Fair at Blackpool in 1956. Walter asked to be there as a Royal Warrant holder as it was Coronation year.

1956   Walter's wife Molly died very suddenly on 23 October.

             The first glost kiln was demolished in August and a twin-chambered electric kiln was installed. The first firing taking place in November.

             The first of the International Spring Fairs held at Blackpool where they remained until 1976, afterwards transferring to the National Exhibition Centre, Birmingham.

1959	Walter married Elisabeth (Lis) Kirkby Thomas on 14 February.
1960	W. Moorcroft Ltd, became an independent company with Liberty selling their shares to Walter, his stepmother Hazel and his sister Beatrice.
	John Moorcroft and Gillian O'Connell of Cumoro, Oxford, announced their engagement in January.
1962	John Moorcroft joined the firm and quickly became responsible for sales, specialising in the design and organisation of exhibitions and the analysis of production.
1963	Powder Blue production ceased after 50 years.
1965	Hand throwing of shapes came to an end with the departure of Ted Burdon who retired at 65. Casting and jolleying were introduced all pieces still being finished by turning on the lathe.
1968	Walter Moorcroft went on a trade mission to Canada and the United States. As a result Ebeling and Reuss of Philadelphia were appointed Moorcroft distributors in the USA. Also the important and influential Coral Hibiscus was designed during this trip.
1970	Last flambé firing following the change from coal gas to natural gas and subsequent loss of vital chemical atmosphere.
1971	Walter Moorcroft went to the United States on a trade mission, Atlantic City to California and San Francisco with a few days break in Bermuda. The Bermuda Lily design was inspired by this trip as was the idea of a factory shop.
	The flambé kilns taken down. The twin kilns were some of the last coal fired kilns on a potbank.
	Moorcroft shop developed after the two flambé kilns were pulled down, the remaining bottle kiln was restored, the surrounding ground landscaped with part converted to a car park. A new sign was put up and the factory received a coat of paint, Californian Sand. The shop was run by Gill Moorcroft. The Bottle Oven Museum and Shop were opened on 24 November.
1972	Moorcroft Exhibition to commemorate the centenary of William Moorcroft's birth held at the Victoria and Albert Museum (2 March to 3 April), later touring the UK.
1973	'William Moorcroft and Walter Moorcroft 1897-1973' exhibition held at the Fine Art Society, London, and organised by Richard Dennis.
1976	Miss Beatrice Moorcroft retires after 36 years as a factory inspector.

1977   Miss Beatrice Moorcroft received the ISO from the Queen at Buckingham Place in December. Accompanying her were Walter Moorcroft and their stepmother Mrs William Moorcroft.

1980   Japanese exhibition of Moorcroft in the Tokyo department store of Seibu opened in November. The display was organised by Tokyo's Ato Galleries.

1981   Walter Moorcroft visited Vancouver and Victoria (British Columbia) as a guest of the Henry Birks organisation to support a promotion.

1983   Recession bites at Moorcroft. A large overdraft with the bank compounded by high interest rates and slow sales meant that the financial situation was dire.

1984   Walter Moorcroft, in the hope of finding a saviour for the pottery, contacted the Roper family, who ran the Churchill Pottery, knowing that they wanted to diversify their mass production earthenware business.

       John Moorcroft becomes managing director.

1986   The Roper Brothers were not able to make a go of Moorcroft Pottery. On 16 September with 24 hours remaining John Moorcroft, managing director, finally found buyers. Hugh Edwards, a Moorcroft collector, and his wife Maureen together with Richard Dennis, a specialist Art Pottery dealer, and his wife Sally Dennis (Tuffin) agreed to buy 76% of the shares (70% of the Roper shares and 6% of John Moorcroft's shares) with John Moorcroft and his wife Gill having 24%.

1987   Walter Moorcroft retired in March designing five new patterns – Pineapple Plant, Chestnut, Tulip, Maize and Wild Arum all in limited editions just prior to his departure. Walter became a consultant to the pottery and handed over the art work to Sally Dennis.

       Launch of the Moorcroft Collectors Club. Gill Moorcroft takes on the role of Club secretary.

       Liberty's began to restock Moorcroft pottery, launched with a special exhibition and new book on Moorcroft by Paul Atterbury with contributions by Beatrice Moorcroft.

1988   Bottle Oven wins heritage award. One of the last 46 such bottle ovens in Stoke-on-Trent which once had over 2,000. The Moorcroft kiln was built in 1919.
       There were also celebrations for the Factory which had been built 75 years ago.

1989   The Moorcroft Museum was officially opened by Arnold Mountford on 7 June. Present were Walter and John Moorcroft, Lord Mayor Mr. Stan Bate,

Lady Mayoress Mrs. Margorie Bate, Richard Dennis, Hugh Edwards and other VIP quests.

Walter Moorcroft asked to do some art work for the Anemone design on some large shapes resulting in re-drawing the whole range and the same for the Magnolia range until 1997.

1991   Moorcroft Mosaic by Candace Bahouth unveiled by Arnold Mountford. Measuring six foot by four foot, the mosaic is made up of Moorcroft pottery shards discovered two years previously during construction of the car park at the back of the factory where a shard tip had to be removed.

1992   Sally Tuffin is presented to HRH the Duke of Kent at the Life Style Europe event held in Tokyo. Richard Dennis was also in attendance along with the new Mamoura design.

Rachel Bishop commissioned to produce several designs in December following the departure of Richard Dennis and Sally Tuffin.

1993   Expansion of the factory with a second storey for offices and canteen all of which was constructed without altering the roof line of the unusual single storey building which has a preservation listing. This subsequently freed up space on the ground floor.

Work force also increased from 50 to 60.

Rachel Bishop appointed full-time designer on 4 June, during the Open Weekend, having previously been freelance.

In July, John Moorcroft became Vice President of the British Ceramic Manufacturers' Federation.

1994   In January Moorcroft were part of the Great Britain trade show held in January at the Tokyo Dome, Tokyo. Foxglove was launched at this show.

Moorcroft buys Okra Glass Studios Ltd. Company incorporated 25 February.

John Moorcroft became President of the British Ceramic Manufacturers' Federation in July until July 1995.

1995   James Macintyre & Co. Ltd, Leeds, established in January and run by Jonathan Colville and his wife Debbie Colville (formerly Edwards).

1996   W M Publications Limited established in September.

Gill Moorcroft retires after 25 years involvement with the Moorcroft pottery, having started the Moorcroft shop and then taken on the responsibility of running what become an International Collectors Club.

1997   Centenary celebrations in honour of the one hundred years since William was appointed designer at James Macintyre's.

Publication by W M Publications Limited of *Moorcroft – The Phoenix Years* written by Fraser Street.

Justin Emery the Works Manager retires to take up a degree course at Keele University. Rather than retire altogether Justin agrees to become a consultant for the firm.

23-25 August, Exhibition of Moorcroft Pottery at the Thaxted Guildhall, Essex. 'A Centenary Exhibition of the Phoenix Years. 1986-1997.'

31 August, lighting strikes the historic Moorcroft bottle oven in two places although it remains standing. Restoration of the heritage listed kiln and roof to the shop, along with replacement of various electric items and the security system cost £200,000.

3 October, opening of the exhibition held at Stoke-on-Trent Museum & Art Gallery. 'Moorcroft 1897-1997: 100 years of a Living Art Pottery.'

11-12 October, Moorcroft Centennial Dinner Weekend.

Moorcroft Design Studio established, Rachel Bishop as senior designer.

1998   Cobridge Stoneware PLC company formed on 29 May.

Cobridge Stoneware launched (unofficially) in May at Liberty with 42 pieces on show 19 of which sold. A second showing at Macintyre & Co, Leeds.

Kingsley Enamels Ltd is taken over by W Moorcroft Plc. On the 4 January 1999 the name changed to Moorcroft Enamels.

16 September, official opening of the Cobridge Stoneware works or Phoenix Works, Nile Street, Burslem.

Cobridge Stoneware first shown to retailers at the September NEC Trade Fair. It is worth pointing out that half the new Cobridge works is devoted to the production of lamp bases, production having switched from the Sandbach works thereby freeing up valuable space for the remaining Moorcroft pottery products.

Ted Turner joins Moorcroft as Finance Director.

The joint staff of both works now totals 115. By November 1999 the staff level had risen to 225. In 1996, there were something like 75 staff.

The Sentinel Business Man of the Year Award given to Hugh Edwards following a sales rise of a third in 1997. W Moorcroft Plc were also runners-up for the Business Innovation award.

1999   Publication of *Walter Moorcroft – Memories of Life & Living* written by Walter Moorcroft, published by Richard Dennis Publications.

Moorcroft Enamels launched at Liberty on 13 May, for which an exclusive design was created based on a design by William Moorcroft in 1908, 'Narcissus'. Produced in a limited edition of 250.

Moorcroft Enamels are now sold in the Moorcroft Pottery shop.

In June Walter Moorcroft awarded the OBE in the Queen's Birthday Honours list with the investiture taking place in November. After the presentation from Prince Charles, Walter and his family were invited to a champagne reception by the Lord Chamberlain in his private suite in Buckingham Palace.

Launch of Moorcroft's Millennium designs at the Victoria & Albert Museum. December.

Hugh Edwards appointed to the Ceramic Industry Forum as a director. The forum, linked with Staffordshire and Keele universities, has been set the task of investigating the future of ceramics in Britain.

2000   *Winds of Change* by Fraser Street, published by W M Publications

Small training school opened in Hot Lane, Burslem, opposite the Phoenix Works.

Kim Thompson appointed to the main board of W. Moorcroft Plc as Administration Director.

Moorcroft Millennium Exhibition held at the Thaxted Guildhall, April.

Altanta Gift Fair, USA, July.

Allan Wright appointed to the board as Sales Director, following Peter Hughes departure. Allan Wright has been involved with the company since 1987.

Early History

The last years of the Victorian era saw unprecedented growth in many ways. The fruits of financial investment saw the development of many new businesses backed by those who were willing to loan money to the new ventures. The ceramics industry had been through a period of enforced self-assessment due to foreign competition during the 1890s, notably a review of the products it was supplying to its public. The rather unsteady state of the Potteries, indeed much of 'industry' in terms of design had been all too loudly condemned by noted design and decorative art authority William Morris who had lent further emphasis to the words of John Ruskin and even Henry Cole before him. Much of what William Morris had advocated in terms of a new approach to design and its relationship to industry had been lost or confused by his steadfast and rather set ideals of returning to the days of craft skills not only for inspiration but also as a model or solution for the setting up of contemporary practical businesses. Had Morris taken the next step as Hermann Mathesius was to realise and put into effect, namely to persuade industry that a strong infusion of design could be of great benefit in the long run, his words and efforts might have bourne greater fruit than they did. As it is Morris can be seen to have stemmed the flow of 'good design' by refusing to involve industry in his later speeches and writing.

One thing that can be said about many practitioners of the Arts & Crafts Movement is that to most, it, meaning the 'Movement,' was a convenient peg on which to hang their wares having picked out by which of the 'rules' or 'tenants' laid down by Morris they 'choose' to be guided. In terms of pottery the 'ideal' as laid down by Morris meant setting up a pottery in a rural environment, using local labour, local materials for making, decorating and modelling, glazing and firing and methods of making that gave those involved the honesty and love of labour. In other words very much as the potters in mediaeval times and some still practising country potteries, were doing, only without the decorative inspiration as advocated by Morris. As already mentioned many of the potteries that exhibited in the Arts & Crafts exhibitions or promoted and advertised their wares as Art Pottery paid only scant regard to the principles of Morris. Those potteries that did set themselves up as 'true' Arts & Crafts Potteries did not fare so well. The Della Robbia Pottery in Birkenhead is perhaps that best known pottery that initially tried to keep to the Morrisian principles only to fail through lack of suitable raw material and lack of a professional thrower. The Medmenham Pottery was another Morrisian venture, although less well known, born out of the frustration of a founder member of the Della Robbia Pottery, namely Conrad Dressler. The frustration of Dressler was that Harold Rathbone, owner of the Della Robbia Pottery, 'gave in' to commercialism hiring a professional thrower from Doulton as well as importing clay and other raw materials from outside the local area. The wares of the De Morgan pottery were praised and used by William Morris but more for their visual decorative appearance than anything else. De Morgan himself always objected to being associated with the practitioners of the Arts and Crafts and certainly his methods of production, his inability to allow more design freedom to his entrusted decorators and his use latterly of hand painted polychrome decorated tissue designs, amongst other reasons, all make a mockery his of supposed 'Arts and Crafts' status. This status was further erroneously enhanced by various twentieth century authors again with 'appearance' or the 'concept' behind the designs generating sufficient merit; De Morgan being placed at the head of the "Arts and Crafts pottery class".

During the period between the 1870s and 1910s there has been some confusion amongst twentieth century authors over the place and association of 'Art potteries' and 'Arts and Crafts potteries' in relation to the Arts and Crafts Movement. Whilst the Art Potters were inspired by the words of Morris they were not at 'all' interested in the principles he set out as to the establishment of his ideal for an Arts and Crafts pottery. Of these 'Art Potteries' only a few managed to successfully combine both shape and decoration to merit what has been considered worthy pottery. What I am not including in these 'Art Potteries' are those potteries who produced what at the time were called 'Fancy' wares; some of the potteries making such ware openly advertised their ware as such. These wares had their place in the scheme of things; made to be sold as inexpensive wares available on local markets for those unable to afford the higher prices being sought for the 'Art wares'. Most 'Art pottery' wares had the basic reality of 'commercial success' as their watch-word, fighting amongst their fellow competitors for the relatively small middle class market.

Where does this leave William Moorcroft? The Moorcroft Pottery can be considered to be the most commercially successful 'Art Pottery' in the group inspired by the words of William Morris. That William was able to establish his own pottery was due to his previous work at Macintyre & Co and the fact that Harry Barnard had already laid the foundations for slip decorated 'Art wares.' Macintyres', typical of so many other potteries in the 1890s, wanted to join the new and lucrative market of 'Art pottery' wares and employed a number of art directors to instigate an 'Art pottery' line along side the main production of wares, with the director expected to contribute to the main lines also. For sixteen years Macintyres' were able to compete at the highest level of the 'Art Pottery' world, exhibiting in some of the world's most prestigious fairs and winning numerous awards through the designs of William Moorcroft. The commercial reality for Macintyres' was that it was their art director William Moorcroft who was gaining notoriety and personal acclaim, largely at the expense of the firm that employed him. This situation probably arose partially through the mismanagement by Macintyres of the situation, no doubt allowing William too much freedom to do as he pleased, especially on the back of the initial sales success William's designs brought to the firm. This success may have been as much due to the largesse of William himself and attention critics gave to William himself as to the willingness of Macintyres' to let the situation continue. Whatever the actual passage of events Macintyres' felt that their main line of business was suffering as a consequence of the time and space given over to the subsidiary 'Art Pottery' line being produced by William. As with Harry Barnard before him William was asked to leave thereby restoring the decision making to those in charge of Macintyre & Co. After initial trepidation about what the future might hold William was able to establish the potential of a more secure and challenging future through his already well-established relationship with Arthur Lasenby Liberty, more of which later.

William Moorcroft was very concerned to establish a pottery where the marriage of shape and decoration were paramount, where the quality of the product had to be the highest possible and where the designs should capture the vibrancy and vitality of nature. In later years when popular taste shifted away from the direct influence of nature this was to cause problems, if only because of the deeply entrenched expectations of the loyal client base. Perhaps most importantly William wanted to make wares that could be produced in volume and therefore available to a wide audience, on commercial lines. By volume the comparison should be made between a small labour intensive pottery and that of an art pottery such as Della Robbia, William De Morgan and the Ruskin wares produced by Howson Taylor. The marriage of art and industry, something that Morris talked about but seemed at odds to make a reality, leaving it to Henry Mathesius and the Deutscher Werkbund, later the Bauhaus, to put into practice, was something that did concern William Moorcroft.

However, what was a 'commercial' volume production line in the 1920s for a small pottery, which would have been running at between 4,000 to 6,000 pieces a year on average, was by the 1950s considered a minor 'limited' production run for one object. Walter remembers that "when I entered the factory in 1935 the turnover was under 7,000 . . . it was in the top 6,000s . . . and my father was drawing a salary of £1,500 a year that's 25 percent of the turnover . . . plus a commission of five percent on sales . . . So somewhere down the line it was potentially profitable . . . if you could take 25 percent out on one man's salary . . . I mean I didn't get paid for my first three years." As Walter stated in his book one of his ambitions was to get production over 10,000 pieces in a year.

The works that William built was the most modern and revolutionary new pottery of the early twentieth century, the Cobridge Works, in the midst of the Potteries in Stoke-on-Trent. The significance of the factory, albeit a smaller revised factory than William had originally hoped to build, cannot be overestimated. The fact that it was to be built at the same time that the new Pottery Regulations came into force, 1913, under the Factories Act, can only have been beneficial. Of further coincidence was the fact that William early in 1913 married Florence Lovibond, who was by profession an inspector of factories for the Home Office. Whether by fate or design forces seemed to be converging, directing the progresses and future of William in a positive way. Obviously under the guidance of both the architect, who in turn was influenced by the new regulations, and the influence and knowledge of his new wife, William was able to build a new factory that was to establish the format for many future potteries.

The new plans for the construction of the building were very simple; to allow sufficient space for new machinery to be operated efficiently; for the continual flow through of ware, from raw material, through production, decoration, firing and storage, all on a single storey negating the need for carrying heavy trays of wares up and down stairs, which created endless problems and wasted much time. The building could easily be kept free of much problematic dust by hosing down the floors every night and additionally by the introduction of extractor fans in the turning/throwing room. The rooms were to be well-lit initially by large areas of windows and later with additional electric lighting. Facilities such as washrooms and lavatories were more than adequate for the workforce. The simplicity of construction enabled the building to be completed very quickly, William moving into the new works at the end of August 1913.

Inevitably there were niggling problems with the transfer of manufacture from the Mcintyre works to the new Moorcroft pottery. Also with the relationship between Henry Watkin and William became fractious due to some interviews William gave to the *Pottery Gazette*. All disputes were resolved by 24 June, 1914, however, when Liberty's and Macintyre's signed a letter outlining the new set-up to retailers, the press and suppliers.

That the building and development of the Moorcroft pottery was at all possible, was due to the relationship and trust that the Liberty family had in William and the prospects they saw in his designs. Liberty's were one of the earliest retailers to spot the potential of William's Florian ware designs, at Macintyre & Co, taking orders to stock their Regent Street business. Others such as Tiffany in New York and Rouard of Paris were equally convinced of the potential. It wasn't long before Liberty were having specific patterns made exclusively for themselves marked with their own backstamp, adding new designs during William's employment at Macintyre's. Liberty's commissioned commemorative wares for the coronation of Edward VII in 1902 and later for George V in 1911. They also had commissioned presents for members of the family. It wasn't long before William become friends with members of the Liberty family.

From correspondence between Alwyn Lasenby Liberty and William Moorcroft it is clear that the Liberty family had a very hands-on relationship with the pottery, to the point of producing balance sheets, paying for raw materials, paying William's salary, etc. Liberty were also the largest customer which obviously made sense in terms of promotion and development of sales, as well as acting as Moorcroft's London showroom. More importantly from William's point of view this was one side of the business that he did not initially have to think about to any great degree, allowing him time to concentrate on the development of patterns, and their production.

With the support of Liberty again, William was able to exhibit in numerous fairs and exhibitions ranging from the annual British Industries Fair, which became an important showcase for many years, to the more prestigious international fairs. The importance of these fairs, particularly the latter, cannot be underestimated as the achievements, prizes and honours that were heaped on the wares designed by William made the Moorcroft name amongst his fellow potters. Undoubtedly one of the most successful fairs, both in terms of orders, national and international, but perhaps even more so as a promotional vehicle, was the 1924 Wembley Exhibition or British Empire Exhibition. Edward Maufe designed a wonderfully restrained classically inspired edifice, that whilst not the largest stand, that being reserved for the likes of Royal Cauldon, (one of the largest and most successful potteries of the period) it certainly won special praise. The press coverage during and after the exhibition was extremely favourable towards Moorcroft no doubt in some small measure reflecting the amount of interest previously shown in the wares by the Royal family.

The patronage of the Royal Family was what helped to make Moorcroft a household name thereby ensuring future commercial success. For many years, even before William had started his own Cobridge works, there had been Royal patronage but the ultimate and most highly-prized reward for any British potter, namely official Royal patronage, arrived a few years after the Wembley exhibition in 1928 when the Royal Warrant was granted to Moorcroft. This award can be seen as a confirmation of the popularity and success of the Moorcroft pottery, but also confirms the huge success that the pottery had been for a number of years. This success was due as much as to the ever growing demand from abroad for Moorcroft wares as for the home market. Canada, Australia and New Zealand, Japan, North and South America and South Africa were all strong markets for traditional Moorcroft designs, in particular strong colourful wares and flambés.

Even amidst such success Moorcroft, like so many other potteries, had a difficult period in the late 1920s and early 1930s, in part due to the rise of more contemporary design styles such as Art Deco, but also because of the financial crisis brought on by the Wall Street crash in 1929. In many respects, it was the Art Deco style that brought about greater problems as attempts by William to incorporate needed stylistic changes to the normal range of Moorcroft wares brought about cries from retailers and the buying public alike that the new designs were not 'Moorcroft' or rather what they 'expected' of Moorcroft. William, aware of a going interest for studio pottery, even developed what has become known as a 'natural' line of wares where the hand thrown nature of the forms were exentuated and monochrome glazes or mottled glazes were used.

The new designs whether successful or not were added to an already wide and varied range of wares from which customers could choose. It was this depth of designs that was available throughout the 1930s that helped Moorcroft survive. Even amongst the new advocates of the growing debate of 'good design', with elected officials often trying to tell industry what 'they' considered to be 'good design' and what the public therefore ought to expect and even ask for in terms of design, Moorcroft wares were often used as paragons of 'good design'. A noted internationally recognised authority on aspects of Design, Nikolaus Pevsner talking about tableware in his 1937 *Enquiry into Industrial Art in England* wrote that "one of the best contemporary sets, William Moorcroft's famous Plain Blue, was designed in 1913, and is, in spite of that as "modern" as anything created now, and as modern as Josiah Wedgwood's sets, i.e. undately perfect". Some of the requirement of this new, or more accurately most recent, emphasis on 'good design' involved the use of clean lines, minimal use of extraneous surface decoration, functionality, ease of use, etc. It must be said that whilst William was, and continued to be, concerned about the honest marriage of shape and pattern to form a harmonious design, the elevation of his powder blue range onto a pedestal of the 'good design' lobby must have seemed a little fortuitous. A few years later William was to make much use of this much this position to develop an ivory monochrome coloured 'Utility' range for the government's Austerity programme, of tableware largely evolved from the powder blue wares.

The development of the relationships with American and Canadian retailers and importers such as Crest & Co of Chicago and T Eaton of Canada become of vital importance to Moorcroft. Crest & Co in 1937 wanted lampbases and ordered four different types, two with a special version of the Fuchsia design with a yellow flambé glaze. As a consequence more business related to lampbases with regular patterns was developed in America and it was largely because of such orders that Moorcroft were able to continue in production during the War. Moorcroft Pottery was saved from becoming a government storage facility or such like, instead being able, with a much reduced staff, to continue working to fill the foreign orders and develop others all in an effort to help the revenues of the government. Because of such activity at the pottery during the war years, Moorcroft, like so many other firms was able to survive, but only just, it would appear that the personal toll on William was great. William, anxious to keep the works going during the lean times of the war, had to find the right raw materials for making, decorating and firing the wares with the inevitable interruption to normal supplies.

During the autumn of 1945 William was taken ill, his son Walter being allowed to return from the army to continue to look after the works. On 14 October, shortly after Walter had returned, William died leaving Walter to run the pottery.

The Pre-War Wares

Moorcroft has previously been assessed by pattern, chronology and decorative treatments but can equally be reviewed by the transitions that commercial reality brought to bear on the design developments over the years, taking into account tastes, high street fashion, and economic and social conditions. Comparison of contemporary wares produced by other potteries is also a valid way of charting the waxing and waning of their popularity. In this instance we see that William's work at Macintyre's was to a certain extent devoid of any financial constraints or impositions, being merely a department within a larger company. The concerns for those running Macintyres were, however, to become a reality for William when he was running his own pottery. The level of praise and success William achieved in the first few years, from 1897-98 through to 1904-05 and during the next decade almost certainly allowed him to be even more creative, spending more of his time producing a high standard and quality of wares, certainly supported, to some extent, by the standard production wares of Macintyre's. The sort of things that Macintyre's specialised in were commercial pottery and porcelain such as; chemical and sanitary wares, architectural fittings, tiles, door furniture and tablewares. Some of the commercial realities of design for a competitive pottery were apparently brought to bear during William's latter years with Macintyre's when the volume of tube-lining diminished in the new designs. Part of the reason for the more conservative designs from around 1905 was due to the shift away from exotic, colourful and rich pattern designs of the Gesso Faience wares of the 1890s towards a new and more reserved Edwardian style based on the simplicity and elegance of classical patterning along with the change of palette and emphasis inherent with the style.

Early sketches and designs by William show his concerns for the use of nature, plants and organic forms reflecting the contemporary interest shown inn the mass of new books, pamphlets and lectures on the subject. William was concerned that the surface pattern design should not merely be seen or used as a canvas to wrap around a pot, the shape being subservient to the decoration. On some of these early sketches William has written the original inspiration for the some of shapes, such as Chinese, in other cases the shapes themselves show obvious affinities to Middle Eastern, Turkish, Persian, Moorish, Classical and Etruscan forms. Equally the format of some of the patterns shows an interest in Persian, Isnik and Oriental designs with flowerheads surrounded by elongated foliage, insects in flight amongst flowers, carp amongst seaweed and some bold stylisation of flowers. Even the simple naturalistic use of flowers against plain grounds owes much to Japanese design sources, even more so with some of William's later designs. Yet all of his early designs used English flowers and nature, which obviously had an immediate appeal to the indigenous population. It would be wrong to assume/attach Art Nouveau links to the designs of William Moorcroft. Not only would William have loathed such a link but such an association merely through the likeness of the use 'sinuous flowing lines' or 'organic' forms is to disregard William's true love of, and inspiration from, nature.

One should not forget that during these years at Macintyres William was also responsible for other 'ordinary' tableware ranges as indicated in retail catalogues of the period; examples include the Aurelian wares, which were decorated with transfer prints and on-glaze enamel, and Dura ware, amongst others. It was perhaps these wares, due to the decorative techniques involved, which were produced in volume, that the relationship between William and Henry Watkins, William's managing director, started to fade. These wares would have taken up a great deal of space in the Macintyre kilns, along with the more lavishly decorated Florian wares, but do not seem to have been great commercial sellers. The issue of the amount/volume of kiln space being taken up by William's designs compared to the 'standard wares' of Macintyres' was what certainly appears to have brought about the demise of William as art director.

These standard wares had to survive in what was the most competitive and high volume end of the pottery market. There were specialist manufactures such as Sadler's who only made teapots, but made them in high volume and sold them at lowest cost, against whom they had to compete. Finding a niche in this market was difficult as William's reputation was based on his relatively exclusive and expensive wares and exhibition pieces, yet at the same time this reputation enabled William to develop relationships with retailers and then create new lines on the strength of orders and commissions. As has already been expressed the most important, indeed vital, relationship that William had, both at Macintyre's and later, was with the Liberty family. This is not to say that other relationships such as that with the Marshall, Field company of Chicago, Tiffany of New York, and T. Eaton of Canada were not important but they were not to have the input into the whole development and direction of William's work that the Liberty family was to have.

His reputation secure, William was able to create numerous new designs from 1904-05 for the next ten years or so, many of them taking into account more commercial aspects such as a need to produce a greater volume of ware with a greater variety of shapes and hence wider price banding, enabling a greater proportion of those interested in his wares to afford at least some of the smaller pieces. To a certain extent this 'rationalisation' of his designs or his increasing awareness of the need for more commercial designs, came about due to the pressure of fulfilling orders as demand for his wares outstripped the rate at which such lavishly decorated wares could be produced. Production of such hand crafted wares could not be increased overnight as the skills, (tube-lining and painting being the most specialist) required months of training to get to the standards needed.

Many of these new designs reflected the changes in taste and style in home furnishings, towards the lighter, airy and more elegant simplicity of the Edwardian period, leading up to the war. There was still a good demand for the stronger palette which reflecting interest from abroad, particularly Canada and the USA. Swags, roses, garlands, Celtic motives and geometric repetition become the order of the day on the home market, all set in a simple and apparent style with a paler lighter palette to which William added touches of gold. William also developed iridescent lustre glazes which were becoming more and more popular amongst potters and particularly amongst glass manufacturers following the discovery of ancient Roman/Etruscan glass in numerous archaeological sites where iridescent glass was brought out of the earth. It was discovered many years later that the iridescent effect on the glass was brought about by being buried in the earth for centuries, the acids and chemicals in the soil affecting the surface of the glass over time making it appear iridescent.

The prevalent Adam revival style in English interiors saw the introduction of what have become known as the Eighteen Century pattern, Rose Garland, later panelled Florian designs as well as those on cream and/or pale grounds and the later Bara Ware and Tudor Rose with some of the above patterns appearing in various colourways as well as on celadon grounds.

During this period, competition came from the numerous Art Potteries that had grown due to economic success and heightened purchasing power of a new middle class. Amongst the immediate competitors for Moorcroft were the new and highly acclaimed Pilkington's Royal Lancastrian lustre ware being produced again as a separate and largely funded art department within a larger commercial pottery, Royal Doulton stonewares and flambé wares, the Ruskin wares of Howson Taylor, even to an extent the wares of C. H. Brannan, Shelley, Wood & Sons and Bretby. The most immediate competitor would seemingly have been Harry Barnard following his move and elevation to Art Director at Wedgwood's. Harry Barnard either took with him some of slip-trailers he had trained or quickly trained new people to carry out his designs as Barnard continued to produce new slip-trailed designs at Wedgwood for a few years following his departure from Macintyre in 1897. As it transpired the Barnard designs did not achieve any success at Wedgwood. With the ending of the slip-trailed designs at Wedgwood, Harry contacted Frederick Rhead asking him if he could find a place for the girls he had trained up, Rhead who had on at least two occasions written extolling the virtues of his friend Harry Barnard and the decorative slip technique he used, took Harry up on his offer. At the time Rhead was working as art director for Wood's here he quickly developed a new range of wares, Elers wares which included tube-lined pattern outlines.

Minton's new Secessionist ware range, designed by John Wadsworth and L. V. Solon from 1903-04, were more direct competitors through the use of the same technique of tube-lining. Also later Charlotte Rhead was to develop wares for Wood's, where her father had been art director, using the same technique.

The use of raised lines to either separate colour or delineate the edge or structure of a design was used by many pottery manufacturers especially in the tile industry. Commercial production of tiles using the dust pressed method enabled raised line designs to be easily incorporated into the process, thereby cutting out a process of decoration. Tube-lining as a part of the decorative process on tiles, although far more labour intensive and slower, was used by many manufacturers during this period, the 'hand' process seemingly adding to the marketing as well as the cost. Many other utility ware pottery manufacturers also used raised lines to form pattern outlines again the use of this moulded technique meaning that more mass-production was possible. Royal Winton and George Cartlidge working for Hancock amongst them. The latter produced designs that have a similar look to those of William Moorcroft (they were both inspired by nature) with George's designs often taken more literally with a twist of Art Nouveau inspiration mixed with Middle Eastern.

Throughout this period it was always William's designs that were the leaders of the field, winning international awards, being sold in major international retailers, gaining Royal approval and critical praise nationally and internationally. Starting a new factory even with the success and reputation that William had must have been an arduous event. With the factory up and running and new partnership developed, William had to get used to the idea of running a commercially successful pottery for which he was now accountable. Gone was the cushioning of the Macintyre works where accountability was of less concern. 1913 was a new beginning for William at the Cobridge works, he was aided by the guidance of Alwyn Lasenby Liberty who realised that to make a commercial success of the pottery 'bread and butter' lines would have to be introduced involving less skilled labour, faster methods of production and greater turnover. It seems that it was at Alwyn's suggestion, perhaps as a result of developing tea wares and related wares for the Liberty tearooms, that William developed the Powder Blue or Moorcroft Blue wares. It was this line of wares that were to become so successful for the Moorcroft pottery remaining in production until 1963.

It is also noticeable that other 'simplified' wares were being produced at this time including as the monochrome lustres and simple naturalistic wares as well as the panelled fruit and flower wares with their stencil outlined panels, adding to the de-skilling processes. The stencilled technique was apparently introduced as a consequence of the War and the subsequent loss of skilled labour. The development of flambé glazes was something that reflects the contemporary interest of fellow potters such as Howson Taylor, Bernard Moore and William Burton and was to prove of great importance to the both the sales of the pottery and the stature of William. The flambé glazes were to be further developed by William's son Walter as will be seen later. William whilst revelling in the unpredictable nature of the flambé firing sometimes fired items several times in order to achieve a certain look, something Walter was to experiment with later on, realising that misfired or blemished normal wares could often be salvaged for sale through the application of a flambé glaze and then re-fired, as opposed to pure flambé wares where the surface effect is dependent on the glaze itself.

Many of William's patterns at this time seem to have become simplified in terms of the percentage of tube-lining to the painting, thereby creating a better relationship or throughput rate to the kiln. Some of the early Florian ware designs would have entailed a great deal more time spent tube-lining a piece than they required in terms of painting. This would have created an imbalance in the work rate of the paintresses comparative to the tube-liners which would have affected wages. (Methods of calculating wages during these years and up to the time Walter Moorcroft began to run the pottery seem to have been very ad hoc, as with much of the rest of the industry.) By the 1920s designs such as Pomegranate, Pansy, Hazeldene, Moonlit Blue and Claremont had become very popular accounting for a high proportion of the output of the pottery. Each of these designs involved a relatively good rate of tube-lining to painting. Other designs such as Cornflower and Spanish with their rich, exotic colours were also very popular but almost certainly involved more time spent tube-lining each piece. Of course, the ratio of time spent tube-lining a piece as opposed to painting is not as straightforward as it might appear as the number of tube-liners employed compared to paintresses adds another factor into the daily or weekly schedule as well as the build-up or back log of green ware (unfired ware) that could be built up in the 'green room.'

Quite how William was able to keep going during the coal strikes of the 1920s and the financial crash of 1929 is difficult to tell. According to Walter Moorcroft, Moorcroft pottery was no different to many other small firms, all of whom had to scurry around finding coal in sufficient quantities to enable a single firing to be successful. The continuing success in getting orders from foreign markets enabled William to carry on some form of business whilst many other small firms without such orders suffered or closed altogether. The 1920s were without doubt some of William's most successful years in terms of critical acclaim; the pinnacle of his achievement undoubtedly being the success of his stand at the 1924 Wembley Exhibition or British Empire Exhibition. He also received validation from the Royal Family, eventually receiving what to him was perhaps his greatest achievement, being accorded the Royal Warrant in 1928.

The following decade was not to prove so successful for William; indeed the 1920s showed some of the failings that were to point to the struggles of the post-war years. William, in an effort to 'modernise' and keep abreast of the changing high street fashions in the 1920s, added some motifs and new designs that did not have much impact on the market, at least as far as Moorcroft sales were concerned. Art Deco motifs such as banding with repeated chevron or fish scale motifs were introduced. In the early 1930s abstracted or heavy styling of patterns were introduced, specifically the Yacht pattern, stylised peacock feather design, as well as the simplification of patterns, Waving Corn, Honesty, Orange and Blossom all fall into this group. The colour palette also changed, becoming less complicated and paler, the more exotic and rich patterns, including flambé wares, and associated palettes being reserved for export orders where demand was still strong. Matt grounds were used more and more on patterns such as Fish, Waving Corn, Dawn Landscape and other landscape designs.

This is not to say that a number of highly successful designs were not introduced during the late 1920s and 1930s. Autumn Leaves, for example, sometimes known as Berries and Leaves, proved to be extremely popular nationally and internationally. This design, as Walter Moorcroft remembers, was created mainly as a vehicle for flambé and later came in for the full variety of colour palettes and treatments which applied to many patterns. Anemone (introduced in about 1938) and Freesia (introduced in about

The Moorcroft stand designed by Edward Maufe for the British Empire Exhibition held at Wembley in 1924. The four recesses containing Moonlit Blue vases all signed for the occasion and the cabinets between the arches can now be found in the Moorcroft Museum.

1935) were other highly successful patterns in true Moorcroft spirit. The Freesia design occasionally used slip as a decorative element in the design as background between the leaves. By the end of the 1930s the number of designs that were available together with the various colourways and glaze treatments available was quite astounding. An indication of the sudden surge of new designs from the 1920s compared with the 1930s can be seen by looking at the lists of Moorcroft patterns in this book.

One of the least successful ranges at this time was the 'studio' line or 'Natural ware' that was introduced in the late 1930s in response to increased competition from the growing group of studio potters, who were competition for the small commercial potteries. The 'natural' look of these wares with irregular shapes and monochrome and/or graduated two tone glazes did not have any response from the home or export market, the wares being too far removed from anything that a potential purchaser or even retailer expected of 'Moorcroft'. This problem was to become an issue again, this time for Walter, in the post-war period.

The issue of the design was only one part of the problem. In addition there was not as much expendable money available amongst the middle and upper classes that made up the traditional Moorcroft clientele. Added to which was a heavily competitive market place. International fairs of the type that had more or less made William's reputation in the first two decades of the twentieth century were no less significant but perhaps held less significance, if anything highlighting the new emerging simplicity of modern designs. William, aware of the growing competitive home markets, responded by throwing open the pattern books, more than trebling the introduction of new patterns, up-dating some older designs, and making patterns available in numerous colourways. Pieces continued to be ordered by silversmiths and platers continuing a business that had been established many years for. New shapes started to be made to fulfil orders especially for tablewares.

William had achieved his ambition of creating a successful international commercial art pottery business, crossing the divide unbridged by any previous art pottery or indeed similar crafts business. Many new potteries were established in the early years of the twentieth century, usually within a former pottery, the old kilns being brought back into action along with all the other remaining machines, slip room, decorators rooms, etc. William dared to be different from the very beginning. It was always his intention to build a new 'modern' pottery where the processes of production would be able to work at their most efficient. The resultant building was quite revolutionary at the time and in many respects remains so today, after further development over the years. That one man was responsible for the running of such a business, overseeing 'all' aspects of the business by his own methods is perhaps all the more remarkable. However, it was the nature of the man who, like many of his contemporaries in the Art Pottery world, wanted to keep all the secrets of his success, namely the recipes for the glazes and perhaps the body, largely secret, for fear of imitators from abroad. This was something of much concern, repeatedly reported in contemporary trade journals in the early years of the twentieth century. In hindsight such a dogged determination to be in charge of every aspect in the running of such a successful business was detrimental to the continued and future success of the business, even though it might have appeared that all was well. That aside, the designs William produced which had enabled him to establish his own pottery carried on gaining praise nationally and internationally, winning awards and prizes across Europe and North America.

It was this mantle that William's son Walter had to shoulder and to do so a great deal sooner and more suddenly than he might otherwise have expected.

Moorcroft was Moorcroft . . .

Walter Moorcroft initially joined the firm in 1937 after graduating from school. Even at this time his father, William, was not a well man, suffering the consequences of years of running the pottery by himself. The period between 1937 and 1945 is very much a period of transition with Walter learning directly from William (if mostly from the sidelines) the business of the pottery – as well as developing his own character through his time in the services. Walter was soon to realise that the pottery was run like no other, William having developed his own highly personalised way of coping with the daily routine which was soon imbedded in Walter. An account of this period, especially the more personal side of his life, is best left to Walter himself as expressed in his book *Memories of Life and Living*.

The cessation of violence at the end of the war did not immediately bring a return of the decorated wares of the pre-war years. Britain needed money to pay for its efforts during the war and to repay loans taken from the United States. Once life had begun to return to some sort of normal pattern with the wheels of industry once again turning and the land recultivated to full use, all efforts were directed toward building export markets and to the revenue that entailed. Imports were kept to a minimum with only essential basic materials. Gradually, however, the restrictions were lifted. In the meantime Walter found that there was a very healthy demand for their export rejects which he allocated to the small family owned retailers who were his traditional customers.

There were two important exhibitions during this period, "Britain can Make it" in 1947 and "The Festival of Britain" in 1951; Moorcroft played its part in both of these but unfortunately in the wrong manner. Moorcroft were represented, however the wares chosen and heralded as 'Good Design' for Contemporary designs were the Powder Blue tablewares. The Powder Blue tableware range had been singled out by many observers and officials involved in the design issues of pre and post-war British industry. Nikolas Pevsner in *Trends in Design* was one who stated that "W. Moorcroft's famous Blue, one of the best contemporary sets, was designed in 1913, and is, in spite of that, as 'modern' as anything created now, and as 'modern' as Josiah Wedgwood's sets, i.e undately perfect. The case is similar to that of some English eighteenth century cutlery."

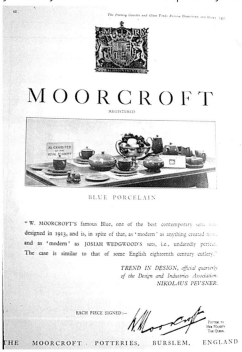

Advert for Powder Blue or Blue Porcelain as it was also known. 1937.

Moorcroft quickly used this in their adverts.

In William's day the acute and detailed management required to oversee the everyday running of production was not as pervasive as it should have been, and this is something that has become even more evident in more recent years. The various tasks and responsibilities that William, and, indeed to a certain extent, Walter, took upon their own shoulders, have, in recent years, been split into specific roles for which several people have now been employed, each concentrating on their own task yet working as a team – but more of that later. The overall direction and planning for the pottery is the role of the management team. Perhaps the pivotal role is that of the works manager responsible for the flow through of ware; mixing the raw materials; and keeping the decorators working without any downtime and without unnecessary costs per piece, to name but a few of the duties.

A later advert for Moorcroft Pottery extolling the virtues of 'traditional' 'hand thrown' wares and yet still 'modern' enough through the 'simplicity of design' to be appealing to the contemporary customers. March 19??

When Walter took over the pottery he gradually introduced various management systems related to the piece rate system (or rather his own version of it). This was a mix of keeping people busy rather than having people waiting to catch up, scheduling daily pieces and patterns required from each paintresses and tube-liners and keeping a check on the monetary value of each kiln load. Over the years numerous incentive and/or bonus schemes were tried, clocking in, timing rates for new patterns on various shapes, varying for years of experience, all such schemes were all dependent on the honesty and co-operation of those involved, and their understanding of the need to adhere to such schemes.

Another of Walter's new activities related to design. At a basic level there were the hand drawn tracings to be done for each design to be transferred to different shapes. This is something that William had always done himself, thereby giving each piece the authentic Moorcroft identity, as Walter calls it. It was only years later that Walter realised that he been brainwashed into believing that this very time consuming part of the process had to be done by him, when it could quite easily have been done by the head paintress. Entirely new designs were, however, his responsibility.

An important difference between the 'contemporary' potteries and Moorcroft during the post war period was in technology. The manufacturing processes at Moorcroft had not changed, indeed have still not changed, to any significant degree. It was the re-equipping and modernisation by established firms along with experimentation and application of new making and decorating techniques, following the war, that enabled the more modern thinking potteries to develop; Midwinter, Poole, Portmeirion, Foley, although at the same time adding to the de-skilling within the industry. New decorating methods included the Murray-Curvex, where a pattern was applied via a rubber bomb to a curved surface and silk screen printing which bought about new colours and bold patterning. More significant developments that affected the methods of production were the numerous automated machines that were introduced, enabling wares to be spray glazed on conveyor belts, or even biscuit fired. The introduction of the Clean Air Act led to the demise of firing by bottle kilns and the rise of new electric and gas kilns; the Top Hat kiln; circular kilns and tunnel kilns, resulted in some standardisation of effects on some potteries. On Moorcroft the change was quite significant. In the late 1950s two of the three bottle kilns at Moorcroft were demolished to make way for two electric kilns with the flambé kiln remaining in production until 1970 by special dispensation. The new kilns, which allowed for greater control of the firing temperatures, meant that new colours could be added to the range but also saw the end of Moorcroft's longest serving range, Powder Blue.

At this vital time of transition for all the potteries, Moorcroft production was greatly affected by the personal tragedy that struck Walter at this point, which he records in his memories. Walter's first wife Molly died and it was many months before he was able to concentrate on work at the pottery. His return was no doubt largely affected by his subsequent relationship and marriage to Lis who rekindled his enthusiasm and helped inspire him to return refreshed and invigorated.

Inevitably it was demand that created new markets and types of ware. In the immediate post-war period the new interest was for a light or white coloured earthenware body with fresh contemporary patterns that reflected the new vibrant surroundings. There was an over riding yearning for anything that was not related to what had been the norm before the war, not only in surface pattern but also in terms of body. Porcelain and bone china were associated with the pre-war generation as well as being more expensive therefore more difficult to sell. More accessible everyday wares and affordable finer earthenware was the answer. By the 1960s this view had altered again, this time related to a change in consumer eating habits and new types of food. Multi-purpose, mix and match, eat on the go, eat anywhere, Oven-to-table wares and durability were some of the new requirements and also mixed in was the movement for healthy eating, growing your own vegetables, being more at one with nature and such related activities. There was, simultaneously, a growing awareness and interest in studio pottery and it was this that some commercial manufacturers became aware of, developing their own ranges using 'stoneware' as the new material. Some manufacturers were clever enough to make their earthenware 'appear' to be stoneware by adding some iron flecks to the glaze and then giving the range a name that seemed to indicate that the body was stoneware, such as "Stonehenge" by Midwinter.

Whilst many of new influences and styles were to have a marked effect on some potteries such as Poole Pottery, this was not really the case for Moorcroft, at least initially. Changes had been tried at Moorcroft but had met with only negative response. When Walter again tried to add more contemporary ranges to the Moorcroft designs the results in terms of orders was not positive. Several of Walter's new designs however were initially praised and commended when first launched especially by those in the trade, but it was the lack of public response, the traditional Moorcroft buying public, that condemned the designs as non-commercial. Had some of these designs been launched under a different label and marketed in a new format to a new public I wonder what the results might have been. In Walter's own words "I designed for a market which was Moorcroft rather than try to keep Moorcroft to a market that didn't want me."

1960 was a significant year for Walter in that for the first time in the history of Moorcroft he had sole control of the pottery. Liberty's, inevitably one of the largest and most reliable of Moorcrofts customers, stopped buying when their house style changed to reflect contemporary taste; a very Italian and plain look and something that Moorcroft didn't fit in to. Walter felt there was little point in carrying on the relationship as a consequence and offered to buy them out of the partnership. This he did, becoming the major shareholder, with Hazel and his sister Beatrice as fellow shareholders.

Shortly after Walter had severed ties with Liberty and had begun to take stock of the situation, his half-brother John Moorcroft joined the firm with sales as his main responsibility. He later took on a variety of tasks, ultimately becoming the Managing Director himself. It wasn't long before he made his impact on the pottery with the suggestion, after carefully working out the figures, that the Powder Blue wares should cease production.

This decision, and consequent reduction of hand skills and labour force, on top of the break from Liberty's and then with the introduction of casting and jolleying and the demise of hand throwing in 1965, show something of the huge transition that Walter had either initiated or had to control after he took on the full responsibility for the Moorcroft Pottery. This period of transition and modernisation was a rejuvenation for the pottery instilling new procedures, new approaches to marketing with research trips abroad to America, Canada and Europe, the introduction of new colours capable of withstanding the high firing temperatures used at Moorcroft, along with new technology and the introduction of many new designs. Inevitably, it took time for the new processes and designs to find their footing and the 1960s home market was not a particularly happy environment for Moorcroft products, unlike the healthy overseas market they had. By all accounts, however, during the 1960s period of transition Moorcroft made profits and did surprisingly well.

The 1970s however, was a mixed era of wonderful distractions and public recognition, a time for new ideas but one in which, in retrospect, it could be said that there was not enough attention paid to the basics of production and the wares.

Promotion and travel seemed to be the order of the day, especially for Walter, during the 1970s following on from a very instructive first trip to Canada and North America in 1968. An early promotional trip to North America stopping in Bermuda on the way back saw the start of a new design, Bermuda Lily and the idea for a factory shop as well as a Bottle Oven Museum originated from the Cannery on Fisherman's Wharf in San Francisco. Further discussions with a representative from Poole Pottery who claimed that they were making more money from selling seconds in the shop than from the factory also helped convince Walter of the need for such a shop. Appropriately, Walter had the factory painted 'Californian Sand' and the grounds were landscaped and a car park built. This facelift for the factory coincidentally occurred just before the 'Operation Eyesore' scheme current in Stoke-on-Trent at the time.

The burgeoning interest in antiques during the late 1960s suddenly saw a renewed interest in old Moorcroft which had the consequent effect of publicising the contemporary products. It also, more importantly, resulted in a lavish exhibition at the Victoria and Albert Museum followed by a selling exhibition of old Moorcroft together with a catalogue, later to be greatly augmented and filled with colour illustrations to form the first book on Moorcroft, all arranged by Richard Dennis. The exhibition was held at the Fine Art Society in New Bond Street, London. This exhibition brought old Moorcroft designs to the attention of many people for the first time, starting a collecting industry that is still very strong today and which promises to remain so for many years to come. Collecting in some form or other was by this time starting to become a serious business, either collecting 'Antique' items or new 'limited edition' wares. The latter was something that Moorcroft started to be involved with more and more although they were late on the scene having had to turn down requests for limited editions on account of the fact that they could only make enough to make a limited edition of 300 to 500 items. Limited numbers in Moorcroft terms were about 30 or 40 items with the first limited edition design, Coral Hibiscus, being produced as an edition of 100 in 1968.

In many respects, it would appear that this lack of ability to make a reasonable 'volume' of wares kept the turn over of the pottery very low comparative to the rising costs of materials, wages, rates, etc. A small work force, still only numbering 30 or so, small kiln capacity and the size of the building, in essence 'space' all restricted or limited the potential profits the company could make. Times had changed in the pottery industry, a factory more or less had to be 'large' and able to diversify to survive especially if its market was attracting interest from those larger companies able to offset the costs of producing more exclusive/expensive lines/ranges by the more cost-effective bread and butter lines. One of the ways for a small exclusive firm to survive would be to make larger, more complex limited editions for sale at very high prices, yet making higher volume mid range wares and ordinary starter bread and butter wares. This is something that has been achieved in more recent years with the help of large amounts of funds available for a burst in activity. Such funds were not forth coming from Liberty during the latter part of the partnership and were not sought in the post war years.

Walter's globetrotting continued in the late 1970s following the introduction of the new Magnolia range which was a huge success, selling in all the traditional international outlets but particularly well in Japan. This was followed by a large exhibition of early Moorcroft designed by William put together by the Ato Gallery and held in the Seibu Department store in Tokyo. Walter went on a promotional trip of British Columbia as a guest of Henry Birks, of Birks stores, Canada, the but then a global recession took hold, hitting two of Moorcrofts most important markets particularly badly, the home market and Canada.

The Post-War Wares

Looking at Walter's designs it is very clear that it was not for a lack of effort or launching new designs or introducing new shapes and colour combinations, that he can be found wanting in any way. Walter experimented a great deal, whenever he had spare time, especially with flambé effects and new colours, the former curtailed only because of government decrees concerning clean air and the latter as a consequence of new kilns installed and the demise of bottle oven firings. Modern technology made many new colours available for the first time while the same time changing others that had been stable Moorcroft colours for years, the best example of the latter being Powder Blue.

The years immediately after the war until the restrictions on home production were lifted were extremely good for Moorcroft wares. Demand was very high for anything with colour after years of 'Utility' wares, so the brightly coloured Moorcroft export rejects were highly sought-after. Anemone, African Lily, Spring Flowers, Orchid and the flambé Autumn Leaf were the patterns that formed the mainstay of production for the overseas market with the earlier designs Pansy, Fishes, Pomegranate, the flambé Autumn Leaves and Wisteria still in demand.

Everything was soon to change and for the Moorcroft Pottery it was the start of the struggle for survival for many years to come, yet with many high points and marked peaks in the fight to keep in business. What had once seemed an effortless continued existence now meant constant re-assessment and planning in an effort to carry on. The lifting of home production restrictions saw the realisation of what had been seen in the Festival of Britain. New materials, modern technology and an influx of new styles and ideas from America, Italy and Scandinavia together with social changes and the altered expectations of a new younger working population meant changes in demand. Moorcroft found itself stuck on a slowly shrinking island, hemmed in by tradition and expectations, limited by its methods of hand-making, rich use of pattern, traditional purchaser base and high-end cost product.

Business abroad for Moorcroft was still good with Canada, South Africa, South America, Australia and New Zealand proving to be especially useful. Walter was able to develop his flambé glazes which were particularly sought-after helping to sustain the finances of the pottery in many ways. As Walter himself observed "Flambé was, in point of fact, a great aid to me in providing designs without drawings. If you substitute the word model for design and you do something in a rich flambé with streaks of yellow or something like that, it's outstanding as a piece. Doesn't matter what the flower is, the flower is merely a vehicle for the colour and that is it. Now when you take that away you've got to go right back to the grass roots, you've got a flower with a fixed colour range and that is it. And of course that is where I realised in 1989 even when I started trying to do the flambé again, apart from the difficulties of doing it, it's function had gone to a great extent because when I was doing flambé we had blue, pink, green, yellow we did have a brown added and one or two odd little bits and pieces. Then suddenly there was an explosion [of new colours created by modern technology] and they could get a whole range of different colours without looking at the flambé kiln. So they could have six or seven different colours on a design take them straight out of the pot [pots of colours supplied by a colour manufacturer] rudely called by some people colouring by numbers. The fact remains that it was an aid to Moorcroft whereby if they had a new design they could work at a colour range without having to resort to flambé firing."

Walter developed several new patterns in the early 1950s Fuchsia, Hibiscus, Bougainvillaea, Orchid and Freesia each of which were produced in a variety of colourways as well as serving very well as a background for Walter's flambé. Some of the flambé effects achieved were quite extraordinary with pieces being left with lustrous colours from brandy or chartreuse to silver. All these effects came to end with the introduction of natural gas as opposed to coal gas on top of the Clean Air Act, although Walter had special dispensation to continue using his flambé kiln as flambé production was at the time in the mid 1950s such a large part of the output of the pottery. The Clean Air Act and the introduction of new kilns in 1956 was to cause the termination of one particular range and with it several jobs at the pottery, namely Powder Blue.

The demise of Powder Blue became inevitable as what was once a useful ware to be placed around the hottest parts of a bottle kiln, around the 'bags' or firing holes (and therefore cost nothing to fire as you couldn't put any other ware in the same place), suddenly with the new electric kilns had to pay it's way and it couldn't. Even after being placed in the hottest part of the trolley, the middle, for the new electric kiln it was still being subsidised by the other wares because it was very labour intensive, having to dip each piece, lids included and then turn off the excess slip from the foot. Once out of the kiln it was then the huge task to find matches of cups and saucers and then sufficient comparable pieces to make a 'good' set. Because of the unpredictable nature of the firing there were many mis-matches, in fact after a number of years there was a warehouse full. Retailers were also getting less and less inclined to order the ware because of the growing costs of the hand-made ware related to much cheaper competition. As John Moorcroft explained "It got to a point where in order to pay its way it was going to have to demand a bone china price for what was basically an earthenware pot and there was a very small market for something of that price". As a consequence Moorcroft staff numbers were cut considerably. Staffing levels during the 1950s were something in the high 40s, possibly about

SPOTLIGHT

Spotlight this month picks out a striking vase which appeared on the stand of W. Moorcroft Ltd., at the Blackpool Fair in February. The hand-thrown shape is tall and clean-cut, with a floral decoration that is simple and yet bold in conception. The softly swirling petals accentuate the gracefully moulded line. These clear crimson tones stand out in effective contrast against the background which gradates in subtle shades from green at the bottom to yellow at the top.

Moorcroft as part of the monthly Pottery Gazette Spotlight *promotional page. The text emphasising the simplicity of the decoration reflecting the shape of the vase and the contrasting palette making for a striking display. May 1958*

48 but by 1961 when Powder Blue ceased, there were 38 staff in all. With the loss of Powder Blue from production there was no need for all three turners, as there was a great deal of turning involved on Powder Blue, so at least one turner went, together with a thrower and the remaining cup handlers. As it was 'the story of Powder Blue' or Moorcroft Blue, by strange coincidence, largely reflects the fortunes of the Moorcroft pottery throughout its history.

John Moorcroft explained the situation regarding Powder Blue in one of the interviews I had with him. "It (Powder Blue) wasn't actually paying its own way. We'd only got a few customers left who were buying it in any quantity, Liberty's, John Lewis, Peter Jones maybe two or three others so we decided that that was something we'd stop . . . I was the bad ogre who stopped the Powder Blue. You see when everybody made by hand it was very competitive but once mechanisation came into table ware, which was happening, there was no way you mechanise the Powder Blue because the little things such as putting the little lugs on the lids to stop the lids from coming off, they were all stuck on by hand, you couldn't get a machine to do that. The fact that it looked the way that it did was because it was dipped into an engobe (which is coloured slip) up to the top. If you were dipping a cup into it like that up to the rim and then took it out, but of course you had slip on the bottom well, when the cup would go back on the lathe to have the foot turned out so there was a wide foot . . ." "It got to a point where in order to pay its way it was going to have to demand a bone china price for what was basically an earthenware pot and there was a very small market for something of that price."

There was also, as Walter Moorcroft was to point out, a technical problem. When the pieces were turned or finished off on the lathe, minute particles of blue slip went into the atmosphere of the pottery and landed on other pots, contaminating them and producing flecks and specks of cobalt on other pots. Walter also suggested that, in hindsight they should have set up another building to make the ware "but as it happened another manufacturer, James Kent or Johnson Brothers someone like . . . a few years later or in the same year did produce their own version but Johnson Brothers were using a hundred and twenty foot tunnel kiln so they were producing thousands

Walter Moorcroft by inspirationally contemporary Whirligig stand, as he calls it, that he design at the Blackpool Fair in 1959. The stand was completed just before the fair by one of the exhibition fitters who was also an undertaker.

41

and thousands of pieces a week." John continued "Yes . . . yes . . . but the other thing that was fascinating to me was that I was sort of brought up to understand that Powder Blue and the speckle was something that nobody else could do and I went to the tech (technical college) when I started to do a ceramics course . . . part-time . . . and at the end of the first year I passed my exams . . . but one of the first things we did was to make an engobe and you made a little square of trials by staining slip with cobalt and they would come in a perfect Powder Blue and I said well so much for the bloody secret that Moorcroft's got, there were a load of students (all making Powder Blue) . . . Yes so that was my introduction to the industry."

The use of coloured slip as a ground colour did not end there however. In the late 1950s Walter came up with more new designs, with the assistance of his new wife Lis, Caribbean being one that used a coloured slip ground. Caribbean was the outcome of a special commission from Trimingham's, an exclusive retailers in Bermuda, which wanted tankards with a Caribbean motif. Other new designs were Marine, Poplar Leaves, Hedgevine and Leaves in the Wind, with other former designs being re-drawn on other shapes. Most of these designs initially created good impressions at the various trade fairs with many pieces being bought from the fairs, however subsequent orders were not as forthcoming as the pottery would have liked or indeed needed. Leaves in the Wind, which Walter refers to as his 'glorious failure', again sold well when it was being promoted at the Blackpool Fair in 1960 but it had no future orders.

All these new designs during the late 1950s and early 1960s were introduced in an attempt to responded to the current trends, the demand for simplicity and to gain a new customer base. Walter designed many new shapes and introduced different solid coloured grounds, features seen particularly in the Leaves in the Wind range but the response was limited to say the least. Moorcroft was trapped by expectation and tradition.

Throughout the 1960s new ideas were coming thick and fast. Walter designed a group of four miniature vases less than 2" high which were very successful. Other small wares followed such as four ashtrays. Table lamps were available with plain silk shades or parchment shades painted with the floral designs seen on the base. As an aid to John travelling around the country selling Moorcrofts wares a catalogue was introduced in 1966. Advertising was increased with Walter often managing to secure a prime spot in the trade journals the *Pottery*

Typical Moorcroft advert of the 1960s where Walter paid extra to have his adverts next to or on the Pottery Gazette index page. August 1960.

Gazette, opposite the index page. Moorcrofts also advertised in the *Ambassador*, *House & Garden* and *Conde Naste* amongst other magazines.

The general trend in Moorcroft during the 1960s was one of change and re-assessment. Signs that the old and traditional ways were no longer possible can be seen in demise of the bottle ovens but also with the end of hand thrown wares at the pottery in preference to slip casting and jolleying. Ted Burdon, the only remaining thrower, retired in 1965 and Walter had been unable to find another thrower to take over the position.

The end of the 1960s saw some success with Walter making his first trip to Canada and the United States which resulted in a new design to fit furnishing styles, namely Coral Hibiscus which was a dramatic departure and great success for the company. This new design was a significant step, as John Moorcroft explained "as the years went by we introduced . . . well, the classic one was the Coral Hibiscus because the Coral Hibiscus was the first Moorcroft design, as far as I'm aware of, that didn't contain blue in any shape or form, up to then everything had had blue somewhere, a bit of shading in blue but in the Coral Hibiscus there was no blue . . . The trade looked at it almost sceptically and saying it's not really Moorcroft they were very slow to pick it up but then it suddenly took off because it fitted into colour schemes . . . because the sort of sagey green colour was a fashion colour and then we did the coral on the brown because brown became very much a fashion colour so we did get involved to a certain extent with fashion but it as only because it became possible to use those colours in our temperatures."

With renewed interest in the wares of the Moorcroft Pottery, albeit mostly the old wares by William, Walter was not slow to make hay while the sun shone. Walter designed Pansy Nouveau as a special commission for Ebeling and Reuss his USA distributors, although he was very pleased to withdraw this design after less than two years having had enormous technical problems with the consistency of the pale green ground. Other commissions included Maple Leaf on lamp bases for Eaton's of Canada and Alamander used on some 30 rectangular boxes. In 1975 Walter designed Magnolia which was to have significant success selling on all five continents. Launched at the first International Gift Fair held at the NEC, Birmingham in February 1976 the design was enthusiastically greeted and sold through the retailers Mutsukoshi of Tokyo.

Walter introduced a range of moulded ceramic jewellery at the Harrogate Gift Fair, which was reasonably successful for two or three years. This was followed in 1978 by a set for smokers, Walter designing the lighter which came in a silk lined box starting the trend for the blue Moorcroft gift boxes.

The enthusiasm for Moorcroft during the late 1970s did not foretell what was to hit the pottery industry, indeed the whole economy, in 1981.

Time of Transition

The finances of the Moorcroft Pottery though not wonderful did not cause any alarm either in their bank to whom they had a steady overdraft or indeed for the Moorcroft accountant. The enthusiasm for old Moorcroft was something that Walter was by now taking advantage off in the factory shop occasionally bringing up a handful of old pieces from the basement storeroom and offering them for sale. The basement was completely full with crates of Williams early designs. What this did, of course, as Walter was later to realise, was to give a false impression of the actual current production profits being added to the monthly sales put out from the proceeds of the sales of the old pieces.

In many respects the Moorcroft Pottery was being kept afloat by the sales of the old pieces as Walter so eloquently put it in one of our interviews, "I think I had a false impression . . . I had an accountant but an accountant will only operate on what you tell him . . . and I had failed to brief him on the methods we were using . . . of a) stock taking and b) assessing the relationship of the sales in the shop to production of stock. In the later 1970s when some of the old Moorcroft started creeping in (to the shop) you could take a handful of that in and put it through the shop and it would have been written off years ago . . . I don't know what he (Ray Heath) bought but he . . . Well in actual fact he . . . at a critical stage he was almost paying our wages, very nearly, at one time . . . not for a long period . . . we were really short at the bank and we'd set some of the old Moorcroft out and he'd give us a thousand pounds or something for it or whatever . . . I wouldn't say the prices were unfair . . . they probably left him with quite a good margin . . . but at that time it hadn't got the universal recognition. He (Ray Heath) in the later stages through the Churchill period, he was very shrewd in that he was ordering that jardiniere shape that I told you about with the straight sides in Anemone wood smoke and he'd order ten in the medium size so long as I signed them . . ."

Moorcroft pottery was already under financial constraints with its bank and on a personal level, as Walter himself reveals in his book. In the potteries the effect of the 1981 recession was quite devastating with numerous firms closing or being bought out. At this time many of the firms were still being run or were owned by the founding families. By 1983 Moorcroft were in serious trouble and approached the Roper family who owned the Churchill Group largely because Walter knew the father Peter Roper, whose three sons ran the pottery. The results of the hours of consultantancy must have been quite devastating to Walter but at the same time he was extremely grateful and relieved that the Roper brothers decided to take on the Moorcroft pottery. Walter personally lost all his shares in the pottery and his position as Managing Director. Had the Ropers not taken it on it may well have ceased to exist, as there was no interest from any other parties.

The Ropers, however, were in a very different business as hotel china ware manufacturers so the fact that even they were prepared to take on a low volume, intensely hand made product, aimed at the extreme high end of the business must have had more than a little to do with the friendship between the two families. If the heart might have ruled the head in the Roper's decision, they must have felt that they could inject some of their commercial skills into the business to make it a more viable commercial product.

Applying their commercial skills the Ropers immediately looked at necessary requirements such as availability of space, where and how to reduce costs how to improve volume at a reduction of costs, etc. Over the previous seventy years the pottery had amassed a huge collection of master shape moulds some of which they continued to reuse from time to time, a substantial collection of wares representing products over the years not to mention a vast numbers of seconds wares. As with any other business there were also vast amounts of paper work, including pattern designs, promotional material, account books, etc. To a commercial enterprise looking to the present and the future, holding on to several rooms full of history was uneconomic. So out it all went, or least much of it. Skips filled with years worth of pattern books, archives, moulds and souvenirs was a regular occurrence in the Potteries throughout the twentieth century especially when more and more of the family owned firms either went bankrupt or were bought out.

New designs were introduced, designed by Walter, the 'Geranium' design, produced whilst in Crete on a short holiday and 'Campanula' were both introduced as raised line moulded wares, thereby cutting out the tube-lining process. Other designs were introduced by Walter but each with little success. In the end the Roper's had to admit defeat. The financial debts of the pottery were not being significantly eroded, new investment was lacking and new sales were not showing any signs of improving. Trying to bring Moorcroft to an unfamiliar mass audience with mass-produced wares at much reduced prices did not have the desired effect. The Moorcroft name and tradition brought with it certain expectations from the public, national and international.

After only two years the hunt was on again for a new saviour of the Moorcroft Pottery as the Roper family threw in the towel. Now it was John Moorcroft's turn to explore all the possible options. It was a telephone call to Hugh Edwards, an enthusiastic collector of William Moorcroft that resulted in a last minute salvation. Hugh Edwards contacted Richard Dennis, an old acquaintance and specialist dealer in nineteenth and twentieth century ceramics including Moorcroft, and his wife Sally Tuffin a noted textile designer and together with Hugh's wife Maureen they all agreed to try and save the pottery. On 16 September 1986 an agreement was reached in which the Edwards family and the Dennis family would own 76% of the shares, leaving John Moorcroft and Gill with 24%. Once again new life was to given to the pottery. The whole situation regarding the taking over of the Pottery from the Ropers is discussed in greater length in the aptly named book by Fraser Street, *Moorcroft – The Phoenix Years*.

The new management team decided to rebuild the exclusive reputation of the pottery returning to the high standards and quality of entirely hand-made ware that were traditionally linked with the pottery. Sally Tuffin was to be the new designer who took on the mantle of revitalising the designs. One of the most fortunate things to happen to Moorcroft during the first years under the new regime was the introduction and employment of Justin Emery at the suggestion of Walter Moorcroft. At such a crucial time with a new and inexperienced management, it was essential that someone with an acute working knowledge of the requirements of production as well as the personality to fulfil the tasks should be placed in complete control of that side of the business. The new management were left to other important matters such as developing new marketing strategies, new promotional ideas and rebuilding the name and reputation of the company.

What has been achieved at the Moorcroft Pottery since 1986 is nothing less than a revival. The journey has been a remarkable one involving an initial six year partnership with Sally Tuffin as head designer, followed by the introduction of a new young designer, Rachel Bishop, who brought back the vitality and traditional expectations to Moorcroft that so many enthusiasts had expected of the company. Markets were re-opened, retailers returned including the much prized account of Liberty & Co, for so long associated with the pottery during its most successful years. A new band of devoted collectors were drawn in by the spell of the pottery and welcomed by a collectors club that has grown remarkably since it was founded and run by Gill Moorcroft in 1987. John Moorcroft in a new role as roving ambassador has travelled the globe winning sales with his enthusiasm and tremendous working knowledge of the pottery and its history. New and ever greater challenges have been targeted by the management constantly pushing the barriers and achievements year after year.

New ideas concerning promotion and advertising have played an important roll in the new look pottery, the name frequently appearing in interiors magazines, house, garden and collectors magazines as well as on television programmes. To keep up with demand employees have increased year after year, the growth in the numbers of limited edition wares on top of the ordinary ranges and other production wares creating extra work. Table lamp production for example has taken on a life of it's own. To keep up with the pressure of demand for new designs every year a new design team or studio was established at the end of 1997. The board of Moorcroft PLC has naturally seen a few changes over the years with Kim Thompson recently appointed to the main board of W. Moorcroft Plc as Administration Director, along with Allan Wright appointed to the board as Sales Director, following Peter Hughes departure.

Completely new ventures have been undertaken such as the opening of the sister pottery, Cobridge Stoneware with its completely new purpose built factory on Nile Street, not far from the Moorcroft pottery. Further expansion involved taking over the Okra Glass Studio Ltd and Kingsley Enamels Ltd, the latter now called Moorcroft Enamels. To cope with the extended Moorcroft family a crèche was established and the business goes from strength to strength.

Lightening has struck and still the work has carried on. A far more detailed account of the life and behind the scenes look at what has been going on at the Moorcroft Pottery since 1986 can be seen in two books by Fraser Street entitled *Moorcroft – The Phoenix Years* and *Moorcroft – Winds of Change*. The fact that this period has been covered in two books indicates just how much has been going on.

Recent Collecting Trends and Developments

The collecting of Moorcroft Pottery has been a serious concern for many people in the past ten to fifteen years. For a few it has been a habit that started back in the 1960s and early 1970s and the value of those early collections has seen a multi-fold increase far out weighing many such investments in stocks, shares, etc. Such pecuniary concerns however have nothing to do with the hours, weeks and years spent travelling from fair to fair, auction to auction, shop to shop and now of course surfing the net in search of yet more pieces to add to a collection. Quite frankly such purist sentiments are wonderful for those who intend to donate their entire collection to a museum. For most of us we aim to buy perfect pieces or as near perfect as possible, in order to be able to sell on in a few years when rarer, bigger or better pieces, which are usually more expensive, that we want to add to our collection turn up for sale. Buying less than perfect pieces is usually something one does until either one can get a perfect replacement or upgrade to something better. In say 'usually' perfect pieces but of course tremendous decorative collections can be built up of the chipped, cracked or even smashed pieces. Habitual collectors will already be aware of much of the above. Taking pleasure in building up a collection of Moorcroft, the knowledge you build up, the people you meet, the stories about the finds and the places to which you went are all part of the story of the collection. The realisation of the collection and the display with special pieces, special often because of how they came to be in the collection, placed in certain places and the acknowledgement of collection is the satisfying end reward.

Moorcroft was, in many respects, one of the potteries that was heralded early on as being 'collectable' along with other 'Art Potteries' such as the Martin brothers, William de Morgan, Doulton Lambeth stonewares, etc. The collector has, as a result, been able to refer to an early exhibition catalogue followed by a book on Moorcroft both published by Richard Dennis Publishing, the information within which was largely gleaned from the surviving family members who were still running the pottery. Because Moorcroft was, indeed has always, been sold internationally collections soon began to develop where the original pieces were in plentiful supply, namely New Zealand, Australia, South Africa, North and South America, Canada and not forgetting, of course, Britain. The auction houses, notably Sotheby's Belgravia, where young cataloguers were cutting their teeth as general ceramics cataloguers along with the rivals at Christie's and Phillips, were all quick to develop sales related to the growing public interest in the Arts and Crafts and Art Nouveau.

By the early to mid 1980s it became very clear that Moorcroft with all its history, early popularity and success was now one of the most sought after 'collectable' art pottery wares. As is always the case, it was the fact that there were plentiful supplies available, nationally and internationally, together with sufficient diversity of wares and in commensurate numbers to cater for the starter collectors on very modest budgets. More limited supplies of some of the mid range wares to fulfil the desires of those with more financial resources together with a steady trickle of the rarest pieces made in very limited numbers enabled serious high-end collectors to pursue their goals. When talking about limited editions, etc, sometimes a hundred or so made before the pattern was withdrawn and perhaps ten or so very large items made for a specific retailer or exhibition or even just a few very rare trial pieces. Because the wares were all made by hand, hand thrown, hand finished, hand painted and hand glazed the source of 'variation' was endless, the flambé fired wares being the ultimate in variation. The fact that the company was still going and now being run by William's son Walter and his brother John certainly added both continuity of design and a historical link to the past, something that the pottery later developed with the opening of the Moorcroft Museum on the factory premises beside the factory shop.

Macintyre Florian Ware vase, c1898-1900, *with violets*, 24.9cm (9¾in), £2000-£3000/$3200-$5575.

Macintyre Florian Ware vase, c1900, *with yellow violets*, 25cm (9⅞in), £2000-£3000/$3200-$5575.

Macintyre Florian Ware vase, c1900, *with yellow irises*, 30.5cm (12in), £2500-£3500/$4000-$6505.

Macintyre two handled Florian Ware vase, c1900, *with stylised peacock feather design*, 12cm (4¾in), £1000-£1500/$1600-$2785. *Macintyre Florian Ware jug*, c1900-03, *with tulips*, 30.5cm (12in), £1000-£1500/$1600-$2785.

Macintyre Florian Ware jardiniere, c1900-02, 29.2cm (11½in) high, £1800-£2200/$2880-$4085.

*Large **Macintyre Florian Ware Daffodil vase**, dated July 1900, 62cm (24½in), £3000-£4000/$4800-$7430. This vase is one of pair of vases both of which are known to have been displayed in James Macintyre's office.*

Left to right: two handled **Macintyre Florian Ware vase**, c1900, with butterflies and cornflowers, 27cm (10¾in), £600-£900/$960-$1670. **Macintyre Florian vase**, c1900, with poppies, 31.5cm (12½in), £1800-£2200/$2880-$4085. **Macintyre Florian ware jug**, c1900-02, with peacock feather designs, 22cm (8¾in), £600-£900/$960-$1670. Two-handled **Macintyre Florian Ware vase**, c1902, decorated with daisy flower heads, 25.5cm (10in), £1000-£1500/$1600-$2785. **Macintyre Florian Ware Landscape jug**, c1903-04, 22cm (8⅝in), £700-£900/$1120-$1670. Two-handled **Macintyre Hesparian ware vase**, c1900-02, with tulips in typical tones of mauve and blue, made for Osler, London, 29.5cm (11⅝in), £800-£1200/$1280-$2230.

Top row: **Macintyre Narcissi vase**, c1908, with a pale lustrous glaze, 24.5cm (9⅝in), £800-£1200/$1280-$2230. **Macintyre Florian Ware vase**, c1900, with stylised peacock feather design, 27cm (10½in), £3800-£4500/$6080-$8360. **Macintyre two handled vase**, c1900, with tulips and forget-me-nots, 19cm (7½in), £400-£800/$640-$1485. Bottom row: **Macintyre Florian Ware vase**, c1902, with tulip flower heads, 20cm (8in), £500-£800/$800-$1485. **Macintyre two handled Florian Ware vase**, c1902, 22cm (8½in), £800-£1200/$1280-$2230. **Macintyre Florian Ware vase**, c1902, 14cm (5½in), £800-£1200/$1280-$2230. **Macintyre Florian Ware vase**, c 1902-03, with a lilac pattern, 15cm (6in), £300-£500/$480-$930. **Macintyre Spanish pattern scent bottle**, c1912, on a celadon ground, 11.5cm (4½in), £800-£1200/$1280-$2230. Tall **Macintyre Florian Ware Tulips vase**, c1900, 40cm (15¾in), £5000-£6000/$8000-$11,145.

51

Pair of Macintyre Florian Ware vases, c1902-03, 22cm (8¼in), £5000-£6000/$8000-$11,145.

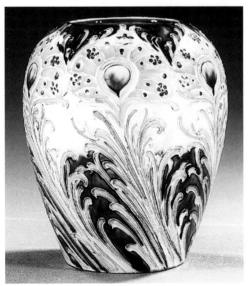

Macintyre Florian Ware vase, *c1900, with stylised peacock designs, 12.5cm (5in), £2000-£2500/$3200-$4645.*

Macintyre three handled tyg, *c1900-02, 13.4cm (5¼in), £2500-£3500/$4000-$6505.*

The record breaking pair of Carp vases, (11" high.) sold for £21,232 on the 19th October 1999, at the Gorringes Auction Saleroom in Lewes.

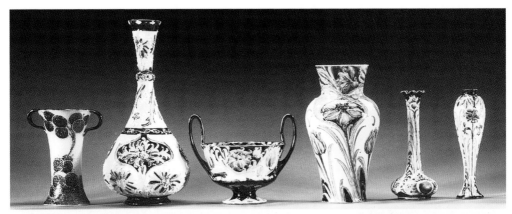

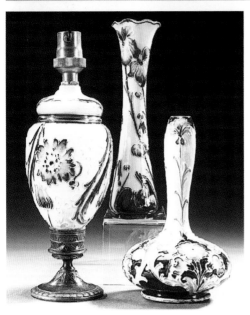

Top: **Macintyre Florian Ware two handled Honesty vase,** *c1903,* £800-£1200/$1280-$2230. **Macintyre Florian Ware vase,** *c1900-02, 28cm (11in),* £1000-£1500/$1600-$2785. **Macintyre Florian Ware two handled kantheros,** *c1899,* £800-£1200/$1280-$2230. **Macintyre Hesparian Ware vase,** *c1902,* £2000-£2500/$3200-$4645. **Macintyre Florian Ware vase,** *c1900-02, with stylised peacock motif,* £600-£900/$960-$1670. **Macintyre Florian Ware vase,** *c1899,* £1000-£1500/$1600-$2785.

Middle: Left to right: **Macintyre Sicilian shaped jug,** *c1900,* £500-£800/$800-$1485. **Macintyre Florian Ware vase,** *c1900, with iris design,* £1000-£1200/$1600-$2230. **Macintyre Florian Ware vase,** *c1900, with Iris design,* £1200-£1800/$1920-$3345. **Macintyre Florian Ware vase,** *c1898, with forget-me-nots,* £1500-£2500/$2400-$4645. **Macintyre Florian Ware bottle vase,** *c1900-02, with cornflower design, 28cm (11in),* £2500-£3500/$4000-$6505. **Macintyre two handled vase,** *c1900, with stylised peacock design,* £800-£1200/$1280-$2230.

Bottom: **Macintyre Florian Ware curtain drop converted into a lampbase,** *c1900, 19cm (7¼in),* £300-£500/$480-$930. **Macintyre Florian Ware vase,** *c1900, with a violets design registered in 1898,* £500-£700/$800-$1485. **Macintyre Florian Ware vase,** *c1900,* £500-£700/$800-$1485.

Left to right: **pair of Macintyre two handled Florian Ware vases**, *c1904, with purple poppies, 29.2cm (11½in), £3500-£4500/$5600-$8360, small* **Macintyre Florian Ware vase**, *c1902, with daises, £3000-£4000/$4800-$7430.* **Macintyre two handled chalice and cover**, *1900-10, £5000-£6000/$8000-$11,145.* **Macintyre Florian Ware vase**, *c1900, with yellow irises, £2500-£3000/$4000-$5575, rare* **Macintyre Carp vase**, *c1902, £10,000-£15,000/$16,000-$27,870.*

Left to right: **Macintyre two handled Florian Ware vase**, *c1916, with cornflowers, 30.8cm (12⅛in), £3000-£3500/$4800-$6505.* **Macintyre Wisteria vase**, *c1912, £2000-£3000/$3200-$5575.* **Macintyre Florian Ware vase**, *c1900, £2000-£3000/$3200-$5575.* **Macintyre Spanish jardiniere**, *c1915, £2500-£3000/$4000-$5575.* **Macintyre Liberty & Co. Florian Ware vase**, *c1902, £2000-£3000/$3200-$5575.*

Left to right: **Waving Corn vase**, mid 1930s, 32.4cm (12¾in), £600-£900/$960-$1670. **Waratah vase** with handle, c1932, 21cm (8¼in), £2000-£3000/$3200-$5575. **Florian Ware Iris vase**, c1900, 30cm (11¾in), £1000-£1500/$1600-$2785. **Persian vase**, 1914-1920, 23.5cm (9¼in), £1200-£1800/$1920-$3345. A rare naturallistic **Iris lustrous vase**, c1908, 30.5cm (12ins), £1500-£2500/$2400-$4645.

Top: **pair of Macintyre Florian Ware plates**, c1902, with iris designs, £800-£1200/$1280-$2230. Bottom: **Macintyre two handled Florian Ware vase**, c1900-02, with stylised peacock design, 19cm (7½in), £1200-£1500/$1920-$2785, **Macintyre Florian Ware vase**, c1902-03, £2000-£2500/$3200-$4645. **Macintyre Florian Ware plate**, c1900, with daffodil motifs, £400-£600/$640-$1115. **Macintyre Florian Ware vase**, c1902, with a daisy design, £1200-£1800/$1920-$3345. **Macintyre Florian Ware bottle vase**, c1900, 25cm (10in), £1500-£2000/$2400-$3715.

*Left to right: **Macintyre Florian Ware vase**, c1900-02, with stylised peacock design, £2000-£2500/$3200-$4645. **Macintyre two handled Florian Ware vase**, c1900, £1800-£2200/$2880-$4085. **Macintyre Florian Ware vase**, c1900, with violets, 30.2cm (11⅞in), £1800-£2200/$2880-$4085. **Macintyre Florian Ware vase**, c1900, with stylised Peacock feathers, £1500-£1800/$2400-$4460. **Macintyre Florian Ware vase**, c1900, with open poppies, £1000-£1500/$1600-$2785.*

***Pair of Macintyre Florian Ware vases**, c1907, with a celadon ground, 15.5cm (6⅛in), £1500-£2000/$2400-$3715. Pair of Macintyre Florian Ware vases, c1900-02, with stylised peacock motifs, £2800-£3200/$4480-$5945.*

Macintyre two handled Alhambra vase, c1903, £1000-£1500/$1600-$2785. Macintyre Alhambra vase, c1903, 29cm (11¾in), £1200-£1800/$1920-$3345.

Top row: Macintyre Florian Ware vase, c1902, with daffodils, 21cm (8¼in), £1800-£2200/$2880-$4085. Macintyre two handled silver mounted bowl, c1904, made for Shreve & Co, San Francisco, with cornflowers, 30cm (11¾in), £4000-£5000/$6400-$9290. Macintyre silver plate mounted biscuit barrel and cover, c1900-06, with naturalistic poppies, 16.5cm (6½in), £800-£1200/$1280-$2230. Bottom row: Macintyre silver plate mounted biscuit barrel, c1900, with irises, 16cm (6¼in), £700-£1000/$1120-$1860. Macintyre two handled Florian Ware bowl, c1902, with poppies, 14cm (5½in), £600-£900/$960-$1670. Macintyre silver plate mounted biscuit barrel and cover, c1900-06, with poppies, 16cm (6¼in), £700-$1000/$1120-$1860.

Macintyre Lilac two handled Florian Ware bowl, c1909, £1000-£1500/$1600-$2785. Macintyre Florian Ware metal mounted biscuit box and cover, c1900, with an Iris design, 24cm (9½in) overall, £800-£1200/$1280-$2230. Macintyre Florian Ware tobacco jar and cover, c1905, with a screw top lid, £500-£700/$800-$1300.

*Top: **Macintyre Dura Ware chocolate jug**, c1902, 17.8cm (7in), £400-£600/$640-$1115. Middle: **Macintyre Florian Ware jug and cover**, c1903, with poppies design, £400-£600/$640-$1115. **Macintyre Dura Ware preserve jar and cover**, c1902, on the Edward shape, £500-£700/$800-$1300. **Macintyre Dura Ware coffee pot and cover**, c1902, £500-£700/$800-$1300. **Macintyre Dura Ware jug with pewter cover**, c1902, with poppies, £400-£600/$640-$1115. Bottom: **Macintyre Dura Ware chocolate pot and cover**, c1902, with blue poppies, 21.6cm (8½in), £500-£700/$800-$1300. **Macintyre Florian Ware salt shaker**, c1902, £600-£900/$960-$1670. **Macintyre Dura Ware teapot and cover**, c1902, on a Kimberley shape, £500-£800/$800-$1485. **Macintyre jug with pewter cover**, c1902, on a Lorne shape, £400-£600/$640-$1115.*

*Left to right: **Macintyre Green and Gold Florian Ware vase**, c1903-09, 25.1cm (9⅞in), £1200-£1800/$1920-$3345. **Macintyre two handled Green and Gold Florian Ware chalice and cover**, c1903-08, £1500-£2000/$2400-$3715. **Macintyre Green and Gold Florian Ware**, c1903-08, £1000-£1500/$1600-$2785. **Macintyre Florian Ware vase**, c1900, with violets, £1200-£1500/$1920-$2785. **Macintyre Florian Ware vase**, c1900, with a stylised peacock design, £2200-£2800/$3520-$5200. **Macintyre Forian Ware cup and saucer**, c1902, with poppies, £600-£900/$960-$1670.*

Top: **Walter Moorcroft flambé Clematis vase**, *late 1940s, £1000-£1500/$1600-$2785.* Middle: **Three Macintyre graduated Dura jugs**, *c1902, on the Kimberley shape, £1200-£1800/$1920-$3345.* **Macintyre Florian Ware vase**, *c1899, £600-£900/$960-$1670.* Bottom: **Two handled Macintyre Eighteenth Century vase**, *c1908, £200-£300/$320-$555.* **Macintyre Florian Ware teapot**, *c1903-04, with Poppy design, £800-£1200/$1280-$2230.* **Macintyre Florian Ware vase**, *c1900-02, 16cm (6in), £1200-£1800/$1920-$3345.*

Macintyre Florian Ware part tea service, c1905, with stylised
Peacock feathers, teapot 17.2cm (6¾in), £4000-£5000/$6400-$9290.

Macintyre Florian Ware vase, c1902, with lilac design, £4500-
£5500/$7200-$10,200. *Macintyre Florian Ware vase*, c1902, with lilac
design, 26.3cm (10¾in), £2500-£3500/$4000-$6505.

Macintyre Florian Ware vase, c1903-05, with blue poppies, 24.8cm (9¾in), £2200-£2800/$3520-$5200.

Macintyre Florian Ware vase, c1902, with cornflower design, 21cm (8¼in), £2500-£3500/$4000-$6505.

Macintyre Florian Ware vase, c1903-05, with blue poppies, 28.6cm (11¼in), £3000-£4000/$4800-$7430.

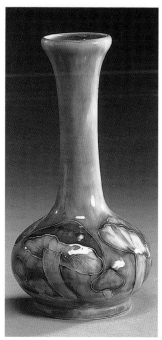

Macintyre Florian Ware bottle vase, c1902-03, 19.7cm (7¾in), £1200-£1800/ $1920-$3345.

Macintyre two handled landscape vase, c1903-04, 30cm (12in), £3500-£4500/$5600-$8360.

Macintyre Claremont vase, c1905, 20.3cm (8in), £2200-£2800/$3520-$5200.

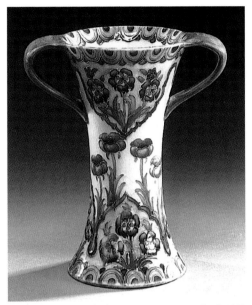

Macintyre two handled Florian Ware vase, dated 1913, 15.2cm (6in), £2000-£3000/$3200-$5575.

Macintyre two handled Florian Ware vase, c1908-09, with forget-me-nots, 26cm (10¼in), £2500-£3500/$4000-$6505.

Macintyre two handled Eighteenth Century vase, c1908, £500-£800/$800-$1485. Macintyre Florian Ware bottle vase, c1908-09, £1800-£2500/$2880-$4645. Macintyre Persian two handled vase, c1914-20, 24.5cm (9⅝in), £4000-£5000/$6400-$9290. Macintyre Florian Ware two handled chalice and cover, c1908-09, £1200-£1800/$1920-$3345.

*Group of **Macintyre Flamminian wares**, 1906-13, made for sale through Liberty & Co, the tallest 50cm (19in), left to right: Bulbous vase, £300-£500/$480-$930; Inkwell, £150-£350/$240-$650; Tall vase, £1000-£1500/$1600-$2785; Small vase, £200-£400/$320-$745; Tobacco jar and cover, £300-£500/$480-$930.*

*Left to right: **Macintyre Claremont bowl**, c1903, 26cm (10¼in) diameter, £800-£1200/$1280-$2230. **Globular Claremont bowl**, c1915, 15.5cm (6¼in) high, £1800-£2200/$2880-$4085. **Macintyre Florian Ware Lilac vase**, c1902, 25.5cm (10in), £1200-£1800/$1920-$3345.*

*Left to right: **Macintyre Florian Ware two handled vase**, c1902-04, with Harebell design, £3000-£4000/$4800-$7430. **Macintyre Florian Ware two handled vase**, c1909, made for Tiffany, New York, £2500-£3000/$4000-$5575. **Macintyre Florian Ware lustrous vase**, c1908, with roses on a lemon lustrous ground usually sold through Liberty & Co, 30cm (12in), £3000-£4000/$4800-$7430. **Macintyre Florian Ware two handled Pansy vase**, c 1911-13, £2000-£2500/$3200-$4645.*

*Pair of **Macintyre candlesticks**, c1907, decorated with floral sprays, 20cm (8in), £1000-£1500/$1600-$2785. **Macintyre Bara ware vase**, c1908-13, £500-£800/$800-$1485.*

*Group of **Macintyre Claremont wares**, c1905-13, shallow dish, 21.5cm (8½in), £2000-£2500/$3200-$4645. Footed bowl, £2000-£2500/$3200-$4645. Vase, 20.3cm (8in), £2500-£3000/$4000-$5575. Compressed vase, £1200-£1800/$1920-$3345.*

***Moorcroft Claremont dish**, c1918, 18.7cm (7⅜in), £1800-£2200/$2880-$4085. Rare **Macintyre silver mounted part Claremont coffee set**, c1910, made for Shreve & Co, San Franscisco, the coffee pot 24.1cm (9½in), £12,000-£18,000/$19,200-$33,440.*

Macintyre commemorative coronation mug, 1902, 9.5cm (3¾in), £500-£800/$800-$1485. *Moorcroft commemorative mug*, c1919, £500-£800/$800-$1485.

Group of **Moorcroft Pomegranate wares**, 1920s, including; jardiniere, £300-£500/$480-$930. Footed bowl, 27.5cm (10¾in) diameter, £300-£500/$480-$930. and a comport, £300-£500/$480-$930.

Macintyre Cornflower tyg, c1912, £2000-£3000/$3200-$5575. *Macintyre Spanish teapot and cover*, c1912-16, £1500-£2500/$2400-$4645. **Macintyre Spanish vase**, c1912-16, £2000-£3000/$3200-$5575. **Macintyre cornflower vase**, c1912, £1500-£2500/$2400-$4645. **Macintyre Spanish jug**, 21cm (8¼in), £600-£900/$960-$1670.

Left: **pair of Dawn Landscape vase**, c1928, £2000-£3000/$3200-$5575. *Middle:* **Macintyre two handled Florian Ware vase**, c1912, £1200-£1800/$1920-$3345. **Macintyre two handled Florian Ware chalice**, c1902, £2000-£2500/$3200-$4645. *Right:* **pair of Macintyre Cornflower vases**, c1912, 24cm (19in), £3000-£3500/$4800-$6505.

*Moorcroft Hazledene bowl, c1914/18, 25cm (10in), £200-£300/$320-$555. **Macintyre Hazeldene vase**, c1903, made for Liberty & Co, £1500-£2000/$2400-$3715.*

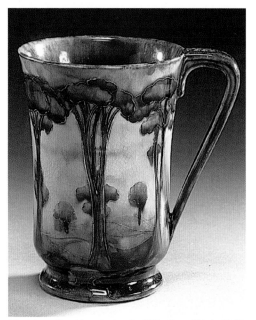

Macintyre Hazeldene tankard, c1903, 13cm (5¼in), £2200-£2600/$3520-$4830.

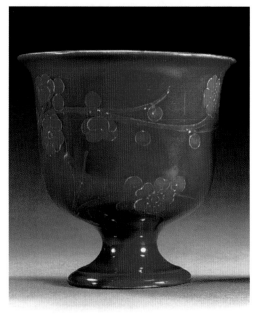

*Moorcroft ruby lustre vase, c1907, with prunus blossom design, £1200-£1500/$1920-$2785. **Moorcroft ruby lustre landscape vase**, c1907, made for Liberty, 16cm (6¼in), £1500-£2000/$2400-$3715.*

Macintyre Cornflower vase, c1910-13, 24.5cm (9½in), £2000-£2800/$3200-$5200.

Macintyre Spanish two handled vase, c1912-16, 25.4cm (10in), £2200-£3000/$3520-$5575.

Rare Macintyre Cornflower part tea service, c1911, the teapot 14.5cm (5¾in) high, £3000-£4000/$4800-$7430

Top: **Macintyre Hazledene vase**, c1912-14, £2000-£3000/$3200-$5575. **Macintyre Cornflower vase**, c1912-13, £700-£1000/$1120-$1860. *Middle:* **Poppies vase**, late 1920s, £1200-£1800/$1920-$3345. **Flambé Wisteria vase**, late 1920s, £1500-£2000/$2400-$3715. **Pair of Florian Ware vases**, c1903-04, with poppies, £3000-£3600/$4800-$6690. **Walter Moorcroft Arum Lily**, c1960, £200-£400/$320-$745. *An* **Autumn Leaves vase**, c1940, 36cm (14in), £1000-£1500/$1600-$2785. *Bottom:* **Macintyre lustre ware Grapes vase**, c1908, £1200-£1800/$1920-$3345. **Two handled Moonlit Blue biscuit barrel**, 1920s, £1500-£2000/$2400-$3715. **Walter Moorcroft Clematis vase**, c1960, 12.8cm (5in), £200-£300/$320-$555. **Macintyre Cornflower jardiniere**, c1912-13, £1200-£1800/$1920-$3345.

Left to right: large **Moorcroft Spanish vase**, *c1915, 46cm (18⅛in), £3000-£3500/$4800-$6505.* **Tall Moorcroft Pomegranate vase**, *dated 1914, £3200-£3800/$5100-$6100.* **Tall Moorcroft Poppies vase**, *1920s, £2000-£2500/$3200-$4645.* **Large Moorcroft Wisteria vase**, *1920, £2000-£2500/$3200-$4645.*

Left to right: **Pomegranate vase**, *dated 10 – 1913, 15.5cm (6¼in), £800-£1200/$1280-$2230.* **Poppy bowl**, *c1925, 31.5cm (12¾in) diam, £500-£800/$800-$1485.* **Moonlit Blue vase**, *c1925, 15cm (6in) £600-£800/$960-$1485.* **Moonlit Blue comport**, *c1925, 15cm (6in) high, £500-£800/$800-$1485.* **Pomegranate bowl**, *c1918-25, 25.5cm (10in), £500-£800/$800-$1485.* **Pomegranate inkwell**, *c1916, 23cm (9in) long, £800-£1200/$1280-$2230.* **Claremont vase**, *c1918, 16.5cm (6½in), £1200-£1800/$1920-$3345.*

Left to right: **Moorcroft stylised Peacock feather vase**, *1930s, £800-£1200/$1280-$2230. An unusual* **Moorcroft Orchid vase**, *c1918, 28cm (11in), £1800-£2200/$2880-$4085.* **Macintyre Tudor Rose vase**, *c1905, £800-£1200/$1280-$2230.*

73

Large Peacock feather bowl, c1918, 30.5cm (12in), £3000-£4000/$4800-$7430.

Macintyre silver overlay Pomegranate teapot and cover, dated 1912, made for Shreve & Company, San Francisco, 16.5cm (6½in), £3000-£4000/$4800-$7430.

Macintyre Hazledene box and cover, c1910, 19cm (7¼in), £300-£400/$480-$745.

Left to right: Moorcroft Tudric Moonlit Blue pewter mounted vase, 1920s, £800-£1200/$1280-$2230. Moorcroft Hazeldene vase, c1913, £1500-£1800/$2400-$3345. Moorcroft Eventide vase, c1925, 21.5cm (8½in), £1800-£2500/$2880-$4645. Moorcroft landscape vase, late 1920s, with unusual pink and cream trees on matt ground, £2000-£3000/$3200-$5575.

*An unusual **Moorcroft landscape vase**, late 1920s, with a Moonlit Blue design in Eventide colourway, 30.5cm (12in), £4000-£5000/$6400-$9290.*

Moorcroft Moonlit Blue landscape vase, *1920s, 15cm (6in), £1200-£1800/$1920-$3345.*

*Left to right: An unusual **Landscape vase**, c1928, a variation of Eventide with pink trees in sombre saltglaze colours, 23.5cm (9¼in), £2000-£3000/$3200-$5575; **Hazeldene bowl**, c1916, 29.5cm (11⅝in) diam., £1200-£1500/$1920-$2785. **Moonlit Blue vase**, c1925, 26.5cm (10⅜in), £2200-£2800/$3520-$5200.*

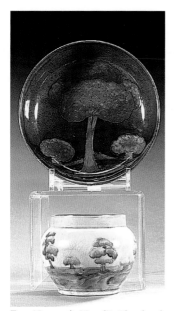

Top: **Moorcroft Moonlit Blue bowl**, 1920s, 19.5cm (7¾in) diameter, £1200-£1800/$1920-$3345. Bottom: **Macintyre Hazledene vase**, c1903, £800-£1200/$1280-$2230.

Moorcroft Dawn landscape vase, late 1920s, between chevron bands, 25cm (10in), £2000-£3000/$3200-$5575.

Moorcroft flambé vase, 1930s, with a Moonlit Blue style design, 24cm (9½in), £1800-£2800/$2880-$5200.

Rare **Moorcroft naturalistic Iris vase**, dated 1919, £1500-£2000/$2400-$3715. **Moorcroft Fish vase**, 1930s, with a matt ground, £2200-£2800/$3520-$5200. A good **Moorcroft salt-glaze landscape vase**, 1920s, 32.4cm (12¾in), £4200-£4800/$6720-$8920. **Moorcroft Dawn landscape vase**, late 1920s, £1200-£1500/$1920-$2785.

*An unusual **Moorcroft lustrous Hazeldene vase**, 1920s, with a copper/bronze lustre, 26cm (10in), £2000-£2500/$3200-$4645.*

*A rare **British Empire Exhibition Moonlit Blue vase**, c1924, signature in blue and British Empire Exhibition, 39cm (15⅜in) high. This is probably one of the four vases that was displayed in the niches of the 1924 Wembley Exhibition (see photograph, page 30), although a number of these vases may have been made from which the best might have been selected. £5000-£7000/$8000-$13,000.*

*Large **Moorcroft Dawn landscape ginger**, late 1920s, lacking cover, 35.6cm (14in), £1800-£2200/$2880-$4085.*

*Moorcroft **Fish charger**, 1930s, 37.5cm (14¾in) diameter, £1500-£2000/$2400-$3715.*

*Top: An **Autumn Leaves bowl**, c1940, £400-£600/$640-$1115. **Pomegranate tray**, c1920, 34cm (13½in) long, £500-£800/$800-$1485, **Walter Moorcroft Anemone vase**, 1950s, £500-£700/$800-$1300. Middle: **Two handled Florian Ware vase**, c1902, with cornflower design, £800-£1200/$1280-$2230. **Moonlit Blue dish**, c1925, £700-£1000/$1120-$1860. **Pair of Florian Ware beakers**, c1900, £400-£600/$640-$1115. **Florian Ware vase**, c1900, £1200-£1800/$1920-$3345. Bottom: **Pomegranate metal mounted**, 1920s, £400-£600/$640-$1115. **Dawn Landscape shallow bowl**, late 1920s, £400-£600/$640-$1115. **Moonlit Blue vase**, 1920s, £700-£900/$1120-$1670. **Moonlit Blue vase**, 1920s, £700-£1000/$1120-$1860. **Pomegranate vase**, 1920s, £600-£900/$960$1670. **Metal mounted Moonlit Blue biscuit barrel and cover**, c1925, £1200-£1800/$1920-$3345.*

Macintyre Liberty & Co Pomegranate vase, c1912, 11.5cm (4½in), £1000/$1600. Macintyre Liberty & Co Pomegranate vase, c1912, 24cm (9½in), £1800/$2880. Macintyre Liberty & Co Claremont vase, c1905, 19.5cm (7¾in), £2500/$4000. matt glazed Fish jug, c1930, 18 cm (7in), £1300/$2080.

Top row: **Claremont vase**, *c1916, £800-£1200/$1280-$2230,* **An inscribed bowl**, *c1916, £600-£900/$960-$1670.* **Macintyre two handled Pomegranate vase**, *c1912, 22cm (8¾in), £1200-£1800/$1920-$3345. Bottom row:* **pair of Liberty pewter mounted Moonlit blue landscape vases**, *c1925, £1800-£2600/$2880-$4830.* **Liberty pewter mounted Hazledene low bowl**, *c1925, £700-£1000/$1120-$1860.* **Claremont low bowl**, *c1918, £800-£1200/$1280-$2230.*

Back: **Moorcroft late Florian Ware bowl**, *c1918, 23cm (9in), £1200-£1800/$1920-$3345.* **Moorcroft Autumn Leaves bowl and cover**, *1930s, £500-£700/$800-$1300. Front:* **Moorcroft Cornflower match striker**, *c1912, with the arms of Trinity College Cambridge, £400-£600/$640-$1115.* **Moorcroft Florian Ware tobacco jar and cover**, *c1910, with the arms of Westminster, £600-£900/$960-$1670.*

*Moorcroft quatrafoil panelled vase, c1918, with flowers on a white reserve with a pale blue ground, 10cm (4in), £800-£1200/$1280-$2230. **Walter Moorcroft cylindrical vase**, 1960s, with a lily bud design, £200-£400/$320-$745. **Moorcroft cloud panelled powder-blue ground vase**, c1920, £500-£800/$800-$1485.*

*Moorcroft Claremont tobacco jar and cover, c1913-16, £1800-£2200/$2880-$4085. **Moorcroft Claremont bowl**, c1913-16, 21cm (8½in), £1200-£1800/$1920-$3345.*

*Top row: **Cornflower vase**, c1925-35, 31cm (12¼in), £1000-£1500/$1600-$2785. **Fish vase**, c1930, with a matt glaze, 26.5cm (10½in), £500-£800/$800-$1485. **Eventide vase**, c1925, 31cm (12¼in), £1000-£1500/$1600-$2785. Bottom row: A globular **Claremont vase**, c1913/16, 17cm (6¾in), £600-£900/$960-$1670. **Claremont vase**, c1930, 21cm (8¼in), £700-£1000/$1120-$1860. **Spanish vase**, c1915-16, 22.5cm (8⅞in), £800-£1200/$1280-$2230. **Waratah vase**, c1932, on a blue ground, 22cm (8⅝in), £1800-$2800/$2880-$5200.*

*Top row: **Pomegranate vase**, c1930, 26.5cm (10½in), £1000-£1500/$1600-$2785. **Pomegranate vase,** c1913-14, 26cm (10¼in), £600-£900/$960-$1670. **Claremont vase with wooden cover**, c1913-16, 17.8cm (7in), £800-£1000/$1280-$1860. **Bulbous Pomegranate vase**, c1914, 14cm (5½in), £600-£900/$960-$1670. **Pomegranate biscuit box and cover**, c1913-14, 16cm (6¼in), £800-£1000/$1280-$1860. **Tall Fishes amongst seaweed vase**, c1930-36, 30.5cm (12in), £800-£1200/$1280-$2230.*

Top: **Moorcroft Spanish two handled vase**, c1913, £1800-£2200/$2880-$4085. *Bottom:* **pair of Florian Ware candlesticks**, 1920s, £600-£900/$960-$1670. **Moorcroft Florian Ware silver mounted ink well and pen tray**, 1920s, £1200-£1600/$1920-$2975. **Moorcroft Grape and Leaf vase**, c1930, 15.2cm (6in), £400-£700/$640-$1300.

Left to right: **Cornflower bowl**, c1913/14, 20.5cm (8in) diam., £1500-£2000/$2400-$3715. *Two-handled powder blue* **Cornflower vase and cover**, 1920s, 16cm (6¼in), £1000-£1500/$1600-$2785. **Persian tazza**, *with Liberty Tudric pewter base*, c1914-1920, 22cm (8⅝in) diam., £1200-£1800/$1920-$3345.

Left to right: **Moorcroft Pansies jardiniere**, *1920s, £800-£1200/$1280-$2230.* **Moorcroft Wisteria inkstand**, *1920s, with brass inkwells, £500-£700/$800-$1300.* **Moorcroft Fresia lamp base**, *1930s, 34cm (13½in) high overall, £500-£700/$800-$1300. Two handled* **Wisteria jardiniere**, *1920s, £1000-£1500/$1600-$2785.*

Left to right: flambe Wisteria vase, late 1920s, 35.5cm (14in), £1700/$2720. flambe Claremont vase, c1920, 18cm (7in), £1400/$2240. flambe Autumn Leaves vase, late 1920s, 31.7cm (12½in), £2000/$3200.

83

Moorcroft powder-blue ground Cornflower vase, c1920, 18.5cm (7¼in), £700-£1000/$1120-$1860.

Powder blue Cornflower vase, dated 1928, 42cm (16½in). £2000-£2500/$3200-$4645.

Moorcroft Poppy design, 1920s, on a powder blue ground, £1000-£1500/$1600-$2785. **Moorcroft Cornflower vase**, 1920s, 17cm (6¾in), £800-£1200/$1280-$2230.

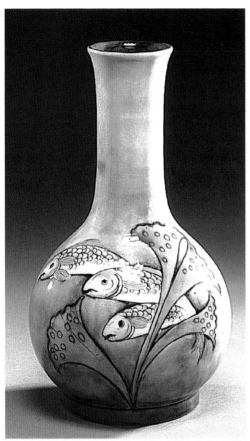

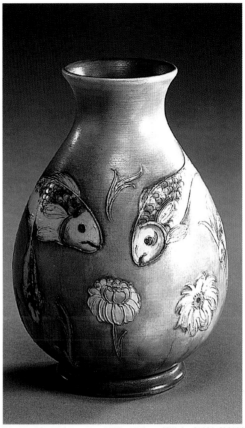

Moorcroft Fish vase, c1930/35, 30.5cm (12in), £2500-£3500/ $4000-$6505.

Moorcroft Fish vase, c1930, 17.5cm (6⅞in), £1800-£2800/ $2880-$5200.

*Left to right: group of **Moorcroft Fish wares**, 1930s, including a jug, £1500-£2000/$2400-$3715. Bottle vase, £1500-£2000/$2400-$3715. Dish, £1000-£1500/$1600-$2785 and a jug, 20cm (8in), £2000-£2500/$3200-$4645.*

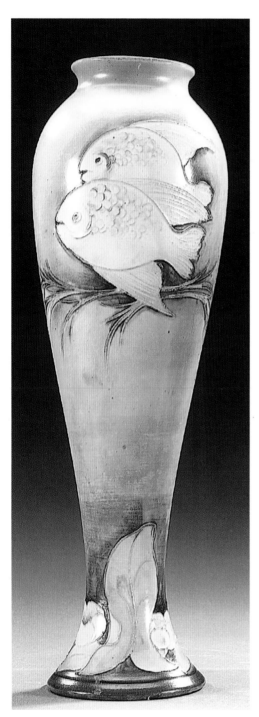

Tall Moorcroft Fish vase, 1930s, 32cm (12½in), £2000-£3000/$3200-$5575.

A **Flambé Cornflower vase**, c1930, 41cm (16¼in), £2500-£3500/$4000-$6505.

Left to right: **Flambé fish vase**, *1930s, 16.5cm (6½in), £1200-£1800/$1920-$3345.* **Flambé fish bowl**, *1930s, 21cm (8¼in), £1000-£1500/$1600-$2785.* *Rare* **Flambé mask**, *c1925, cast from models by Francis Arthur Edwardes, unmarked, 7.8cm (3in), £800-£1200/$1280-$2230. Two-handled* **Claremont vase**, *mid 1930s, 20cm (8in), £2500-£3500/$4000-$6505.* **Flambé fish dish**, *mid 1930s, 22cm (8¾in), £2000-£2500/$3200-$4645.* **Flambé Claremont vase**, *1930s, 21cm (8¼in), £1800-£2200/$2880-$4085.* **Flambé Autumn Leaves dish**, *c1930, 19cm (7½in), £700-£900/$1120-$1670.* **Flambé Autumn Leaves vase**, *c1930, 17cm (6¾in), £800-£1200/$1280-$2230.*

Left to right: **Moorcroft flambe fish ginger jar and a cover**, *1930s, lid matched, 26.7cm (10½in) high. £700-£900/$1120-$1670.* **Moorcroft Waratah flambe dish**, *1930s, 22.2cm (8¾in), £2000-£3000/$3200-$5575.* **Moorcroft flambe Fish vase**, *1930s, 16.5cm (6½in), £1000-£1500/$1600-$2785.*

A **Flambé Autumn Leaves two-handled vase**, *dated 1935, 39.5cm (15½in), £3500-£4500/$5600-$8360.*

Miniature Macintyre Tulip vase, *c1902, 8cm (3in), £700-£1000/$1120-$1860.* **Miniature Macintyre Poppies vase**, *c1902-03, £2000-£2500/$3200-$4645.*

Top: **Moorcroft miniature Dawn landscape vase**, *1920s, £680-£780/$1090-$1450.* **Moorcroft miniature Fish vase**, *1930s, £1200-£1800/$1920-$3345.* **Moorcroft miniature Spanish vase**, *c1914, £800-£1000/$1280-$1860.* **Moorcroft Dawn miniature vase**, *1930s, in an Eventide colourway, £1500-£1800/$2400-$3345. Bottom:* **Moorcroft miniature flambe Fish vase**, *1930s, £1200-£1500/$1920-$2785.* **Macintyre miniature Hazeldene vase**, *c1912, £800-£1200/$1280-$2230.* **Macintyre miniature Florian Ware vase**, *£1500-£2000/$2400-$3715.* **Moorcroft miniature Spanish vase**, *c1915, £600-£900/$960-$1670.*

Group of Moorcroft Freesia wares, 1930s, plate £300-£400/ $480-$745. Left vase, £180-£220/ $290-$410. Small globular vase, £180-£250/$290-$465. Small vase, £400-£600/$640-$1115.

Moorcroft Orchid charger, late 1930s, 41.5cm (16¼in), £1500-£2000/$2400-$3715. Moorcroft Pansies charger, c1930, £800-£1200/ $1280-$2230.

*Pair of two handled **Wisteria** vases, c1930, 20.4cm (8in), £800-£1200/$1280-$2230.*

*Left to right: **Moorcroft Autumn Leaves vase**, 1930s, £600-£900/$960-$1670. **Moorcroft Autumn Leaves lamp base**, 1930s, 43cm (17in) high overall, £700-£900/$1120-$1670. **Moorcroft Autumn Leaves vase**, 1930s, with a matt blue ground, £800-£1200/$1280-$2230. **Moorcroft Honesty vase**, 1930s, £1500-£2000/$2400-$3715.*

*Left to right: Saltglazed Peacock Feather vase, mid 1930s, 24cm (9½in), £2200-£2800/$3520-$5200. **Stylised Feather vase**, mid 1930s, 21.5cm (8½in), £800-£1200/$1280-$2230. **Saltglazed Honesty vase**, mid 1930s, 25.5cm (10in), £1500-£2000/$2400-$3715.*

***Moorcroft Honesty vase**, 1930s, 21cm (8¼in), £800-£1200/$1280-$2230. **Moorcroft Dawn landscape comport**, late 1920s, £500-£700/$800-$1300. **Moorcroft Dawn landscape vase**, late 1920s, £1500-£2000/$2400-$3715.*

Matt glazed Peacock Feather, c1930, 21 cm (8¼in), £800-£1200/$1280-$2230. *Matt glazed two handled Fish vase*, dated 1937, 21.5cm (8½in), £600-£1200/$960-$2230. *Dawn Landscape vase*, c1928, 20.5cm (8¼in), £800-£1200/$1280-$2230.

Left to right: **Moorcroft Peacock vase**, 1930s, 25cm (10in), £1000-£1500/$1600-$2785. **Moorcroft Honesty vase**, 1930s, £1000-£1500/$1600-$2785. **Moorcroft stylised Art Deco Peacock vase**, late 1930s, £800-£1000/$1280-$1850.

Moorcroft Moonlit Blue plate, 1920s, 16.5cm (6½in), £300-£500/$480-$930. ***Moorcroft Orchid plate**, late 1930s, £200-£300/ $320-$555. **Moorcroft Pansy side plate**, c1914, £200-£300/$320-$555. **Moorcroft Orange and Blossom plate**, 1930s, £300-£400/$480-$745. **Moorcroft Yacht side plate**, late 1930s, £150-£250/$240-$465.*

*Left to right: **Moorcroft Wheat vase**, c1930, £300-£500/$480-$930. **Moorcroft Stylised Art Deco Peacock vase**, late 1930s, 29cm (11½in), £300-£600/$480-$1115. **Moorcroft Yatch vase**, late 1930s, £200-£300/$320-$555.*

*Group of **Moorcroft Waving Corn wares** 1930s, including; globular vase, £1200-£1800/$1920-$3345. Vase with matt blue ground, 33cm (13in), £1200-£1800/$1920-$3345. Globular vase mounted as a lamp base, £400-£600/$640-$1115.*

*Left to right: **Walter Moorcroft Fuchsia oxblood yellow flambe vase**, 1937-38 into the 1940s, on a celadon ground, 30cm (11⅞in), £1200-£1800/$1920-$3345. **Tall orchid vase**, mid 1930s, 42cm (16½in) £1800-£2600/$2880-$4830. An unusual **Tiger Lily torchère**, 1940s, Walter Moorcroft has stated that he designed this pattern in 1937 when it was put on a few pieces although it was signed by his father as seems likely in this case, 26cm (10¼in), £1200-£1800/$1920-$3345.*

Macintyre silver metal mounted flambe vase, *1930s, £500-£800/$800-$1485. Group of* **Moorcroft Powder Blue wares**, *1920-40; Jug £200-£300/$320-$555; Plate £80-£120/$130-$225; Butter dish and cover £180-£220/$290-$410; Hot water jug and cover £200-£300/$320-$555; Jam pot and cover £120-£180/$190-$335; Sugar pot and cover £120-£180/$190-$335; Eggcup £60-£90/$95-$165; Cup and saucer £100-£120/$160-$225; Egg-shaped salt and pepper pots £80-£120/$130-$225; and the Acorn cruet £80-£120/$130-$225. Macintrye orange lustre vase, c1910, £200-£400/$320-$745.*

Pair of Walter Moorcroft yellow flambe Fuchsia vases as lampbases, c1948 £1500-£2000/$2400-$3715. Pair of Walter Moorcroft Fuchsia vases as lampbases, c1948, £1000-£1500/$1600-$2785.

Pair of Walter Moorcroft yellow flambé Fuchsia vases, c1948, made for the Crest Company of Chicago, £1500-£2000/$2400-$3715.

Group of Walter Moorcroft Orchid tea wares, 1950s, the three piece tea set £1000-£1500/$1600-$2785. Dark blue ground teapot £500-£700/$800-$1300.

Group of Walter Moorcroft Clematis wares, 1950s to 1970s; Vase £600-£900/$960-$1670; three candy boxes and covers £200-£400/$320-$745; and a **Walter Moorcroft Hibiscus yellow ground ashtray**, *1970s, £80-£120/$130-$225.*

Large **Walter Moorcroft flambe Orchid vase**, *1950s, 33cm (13in), £1000-£1800/$1600-$3345. Large* **Walter Moorcroft Anenome vase**, *1950s, £800-£1200/$1280-$2230.*

98

Group of Walter Moorcroft Caribbean wares, 1958-59. *Cylindrical pot and cover, £300-£500/$480-$930; Two Mugs, £180-£220/$290-$410 each. A barrel shaped mug and cover, £180-£220/$290-$410. Two waisted mugs, £180-£220/$290-$410. Small pot, £80-£120/$130-$225; small coaster, £80-£120/$130-$225. William Moorcroft Yacht serving plate, 1930s, £180-£220/$290-$410; and teapot and cover, £400-£600/$640-$1115.*

Top: **Walter Moorcroft Freesia plate**, *c1955, £300-£400/$480-$745. Middle:* **Walter Moorcroft Columbine dish**, *c1950;* **Walter Moorcroft Spring Flowers vase**, *1950s, £250-£350/$400-$650.* **Walter Moorcroft Spring Flowers lampbase**, *1960s, £300-£500/$480-$930.* **Walter Moorcroft Spring Flowers vase**, *1950s, £500-£800/$800-$1485.*

Group of **Walter Moorcroft flambé wares**, *1960s. Top: small Clematis vase, £300-£500/$480-$930. Freesia vase, £300-£500/$480-$930. Bottom: An African Lily candy box and cover, £400-£600/$640-$1115. A small African Lily coaster, £200-£300/$320-$555, and a candy dish (lacking cover) with forget-me-nots, £200-£300/$320-$555.*

Collection of **Walter Moorcroft miniature vases**, *1960s, 6 to 7.5cm (2½ to 3in) each £180-£250/ $290-$465.*

Group of William and Walter Moorcroft Orchid wares, *two dishes (£250-£350/$400-$650) and the two left hand vases (bottom:*
£600-£900/$960-$1670. Middle trumpet shape: £400-£700/$640-$1300) are Walter's 1950s version of his father's design seen on the
remaining vase dating from the 1930s £800-£1200/$1280-$2230.

Top: **Walter Moorcroft Clematis dish**, *c1960, £500-£800/$800-$1485. Small* **Walter Moorcroft Clematis vase**, *c1960, £400-£600/$640-$1115.* **Walter Moorcroft Hibiscus dish**, *1950s, £300-£500/$480-$930. Bottom:* **Walter Moorcroft Magnolia bowl**, *c1976-77, £200-£400/$320-$745.* **Walter Moorcroft Freesia coaster**, *late 1950s, £150-£250/$240-$465.*

Group of Walter Moorcroft Hibiscus wares, 1960s and 1970s. Top: *yellow ground plate, £250-£350/$400-$650; vase, £400-£600/$640-$1115; white ground vase, (c1974), £500-£700/$800-$1300. Bottom: small green ground vase, £180-£220/$290-$410; blue ground vase, £300-£600/$480-$1115; small bottle vase, £180-£220/$290-$410; yellow ground vase, £300-£400/$480-$745. Walter Moorcroft Tiger Lily plate, c1965, £400-£600/$640-$1115.*

Group of Walter Moorcroft Hibiscus wares, *1960s to 1980s. Top: bulbous vase, £300-£500/$480-$930; plate, £200-£300/$320-$555; bulbous vase, £300-£500/$480-$930. Middle: blue ground plate (1970s), £200-£300/$320-$555; white ground vase, £200-£300/$320-$555; circular lamp fitting, £400-£600/$640-$1115. Front: yellow ground bottle vase, £180-£220/$290-$410; blue ground coaster, £120-£180/$190-$335. Walter Moorcroft Magnolia blue ground bottle vase, 1970s, £300-£400/$480-$745.*

*Group of **Walter Moorcroft Bermuda Lily wares**, c1973-75, white flower on a green ground; plate, £200-£300/$320-$555; candy box and cover, each, £250-£300/$400-$555; circular plaque, £80-£120/$130-$225. Two yellow Bermuda Lily boxes and covers, c1978, £100-£220/$160-$410. **Walter Moorcroft Arum Lily dish**, c1960, £180-£220/$290-$410. Small **Walter Moorcroft Leaves in the Wind vase**, 1960-62, £150-£250/$240-$465.*

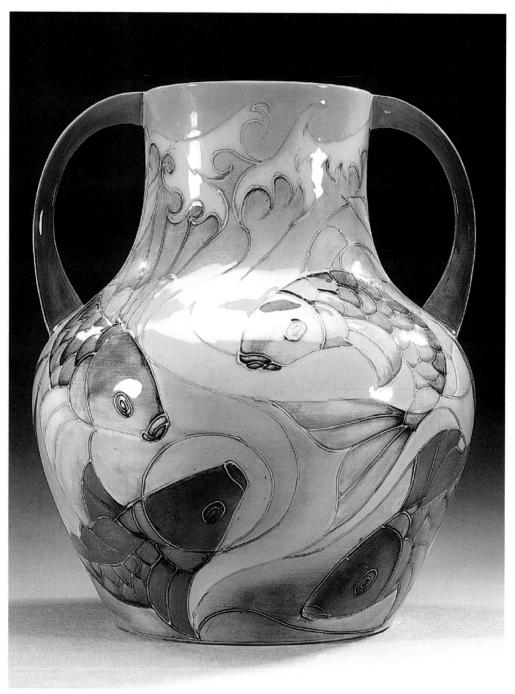

Moorcroft two handled Carp vase, 1990-96, designed by Sally Tuffin, 32cm (12½in), £800-£1200/$1280-$2230.

Walter Moorcroft Marine plate, c1959, 26cm (10in), £600-£900/$960-$1670. *Moorcroft Dragon vase*, 1987-90, designed by Trevor Critchlow, £250-£350/$400-$650.

Moorcroft Reeds ginger jar and cover, 1987-90, designed by Philip Richardson, £300-£400/$480-$745. *Moorcroft Violet vase*, 1987-90, designed by Sally Tuffin, 24.5cm (9⅝in), £300-£400/$480-$745. *Moorcroft Fairy Rings ginger jar and cover*, 1987-90, designed by Philip Richardson, £400-£600/$640-$1115.

Sally Tuffin Eagle Owl vase, 1988, 30.5cm (12in), £500-£700/$800-$1300. Sally Tuffin Rampant Lion vase, 1988, commission for Lion's Den, 25.5cm (10in), £500-£800/$800-$1485. Trevor Critchlow Dragon plate, 1987-89, £300-£500/$480-$930. Trevor Critchlow Dragon vase, 1987-90, blue ground, £500-£700/$800-$1300.

*Top: **Sally Tuffin Balloon plate**, 1988, commissioned by R & R Collectibles, 35.5cm (14in), £300-£500/$480-$930. Left: two **Sally Tuffin HMS Sirus plates**, 1988, for the Australian bicentenary, £250-£350/$400-$650. **Philip Richardson Heron charger**, 1988, £400-£600/$640-$1115. **Sally Tuffin Sunflowers charger**, 1988, £300-£500/$480-$930.*

Walter Moorcroft 'After the Storm' vase, 1996, £2000-£2500/$3200-$4645.

Chronology of Moorcroft Patterns 1894 to 2000

This listing has been compiled from numerous printed and private sources and with special reference to the *Pottery Gazette* and *Glass Trade Review* and the *Pottery and Glass Record*. Inevitably, there is always going to room for error when compiling such listings and here adjustments will be made in the future once any potential alterations have been verified. In some cases the name of a range of ware has been recorded when it was introduced, there being many variations of pattern of subtleties of colourways used under one name. This list has already been verified as much as is possible by Walter Moorcroft who kindly took the time and trouble to make several corrections and amendments for which I am extremely grateful. If you feel that any further alterations need to be made, please do let me know and they will be verified and added, with due recognition, of course, in any later editions of this book. What is almost certain is that there are many patterns and variations of patterns that have been left out, some of which have yet to be discovered judging by the Moorcroft order books.

I should just point out that to differentiate designers and/or patterns by different designers within the various sections, headed with a designers name, I have used bold heading, underlining and italics as a means of making the atypical apparent.

Macintyre & Co
1894
Taluf by Richard Lunn.
Washington Faience by Richard Lunn, Master of Central School of Art & Design.
1895/96
Gesso Faience by Harry Barnard.

William Moorcroft
1897
Aurelian printed pattern. Can be found in numerous variations, colour printed, blue and white printed, blue & gilt . . .
Dura
Cornflower
Florian Wares The first phase associated with Florian ware dates from 1898 through to about 1905, numerous designs being registered over the years until the end of 1904. The designs were used with the Florian mark until 1912-13 when William left Macintyre's.
1898
Full Iris with/without buds amongst elongated foliage.
Violets on tall stems.
Large open Poppies amongst lavish elongated foliage.
Stylised Peacock motif with large eye motif amongst elongated foliage/feathers.
Butterfly border. This refers to the use of a band of butterflies as a border together with patterns such as poppies, cornflowers and sweet pea and was even used on the famous Ship vase.

1899

Wild Rose.

Freesia amongst elongated foliage.

Butterfly Ware. This had a special mark, although not always used. These wares have a solid coloured ground decorated with a band of butterflies often in gilt with tube-lined scrolls and Forget-me-nots.

Crocuses in elongated foliate panels with/without Primroses.

1900

Partial Iris with/without buds amongst elongated foliage.

Iris with Forget-me-nots.

Daffodils with/without buds amongst elongated foliage.

Daffodils within elongated foliage in Art Nouveau style with forget-me-nots.

Stylised Peacock motif plain and/or with dots and/or small flowers and elongated foliage.

Stylised Peacock design with overlapping eye motif with elongated foliage.

Stylised Cornflower design with/without buds amongst elongated foliage.

Early Daisy with groups of flowers in compartments of elongated foliage.

Lavish Tulips with/without buds amongst elongated foliage with a band of heart motifs.

1902

Daisy with/without bud amongst foliage.

Simple or naturalistic Daisy on tall stems with/without buds, on a monochrome ground.

Coronation wares. King Edward VII. Mug designed by Lasenby Liberty for Mr & Mrs Liberty.

Christmas Greetings ware. Various pieces were made with the inscription: "Christmas and New Year Greetings". Possibly a private commission as gifts.

Carp amongst aquatic plants with/without shell.

Tulips, band of flowers towards the base against a coloured ground, flowers on tall stems against a pale/cream coloured ground.

Cornflower, band of flowers towards the base against a coloured ground, flowers and buds on stems against a pale/cream ground above.

Lilac, a band of flowers towards the base against a coloured ground, flowers with stems with foliage against a pale/cream coloured ground.

Poppies and Tulips.

Dubarry Iris tableware design of moulded scroll panels and tube-lined irises.

Harebells, with a band of flowers towards the base against a dark ground, with tall stems of bell formed flowers against a pale/cream ground above.

Seaweed spiralling on a plain ground.

Landscape design. Initially promoted as 'Burslem Ware' by Liberty, later called Hazeldene. Various colourways do appear in 1903/04.

1902-03

Poppy design with purple flowers on tall stems with elongated foliage on a white ground. There are two other colourways.

Liberty style. This relates to a certain colourway.

1903

Claremont toadstool design sold through Liberty. Withdrawn in about 1940.

Honesty on tall stems with a textured surface. The textured surface can also be found over other designs such as Poppies and Forget-me-nots.

Green and Gold Florian, registered in 1903, there are three colour variations – green, blue and pink, with blue being the rarest. This 'style' is a very much pared down and simplified version of earlier.

1904

Tudor Rose sold through Liberty.

Bluebell border. This appears on tea and dinner wares commissioned by Liberty.

Daisy and Poppy design with/without gilding.

1905

Stylised Lilac flowers in compartments in bands with/without gilt decoration.

Flamminian ware. By 1915 production seems to have ceased.

1907

Lustre ware. From 1907 until about 1910.

Rose Garland. Gently spiralling garlands of roses and foliage on a white ground, with/without gilded highlights.

Floral spray design with repeated sprays of roses, tulips and forget-me-nots on stems with elongated foliage and small leaves on a white ground, often with further scattered flowers. With/without gilt highlights.

1908

Eighteenth Century. Swags of red roses, purple forget-me-nots and small green foliage, with/without gilt highlights, on a white ground.

Forget-me-nots in compartments. The scalloped edged compartments of Forget-me-nots combined with either tulips or poppies on a white ground. Often found with looped bands on the foot and/or neck. There are also various colourways.

Bara ware. This design was made exclusively for Liberty and used until about 1913.

1909

Quatrefoil panels with Forget-me-nots, the flowers and foliage within tube-lined large and small panels, with/without additional foliage, on a white ground.

1910

Commemorative ware. Kings College Cambridge – printed crest.

Pomegranate. This design was initially called Murena when sold through Liberty.

Spanish.

1911

Pansy. Early version, 1911-13, with bands of yellow, mauve and red flowers and pale green foliage on a white ground. Between 1913 and about 1918 the flowers became darker, then the ground was painted with a blue to green mottled ground and then a dark blue and/or dark blue and green ground

Wisteria. Later versions appeared in the 1920s and 1930s.

Norton Mug. Made for Lord Nelson to commemorative the Coronation of George V.

Coronation mug for George V. Made for Mr & Mrs Liberty.

Commemorative two handled vase. Tube-lined with an heraldic lion within a shield decorated with fleur-de-lys. This comes with various patriotic Latin inscriptions.

Commemorative vase. For the Coronation of George V, tube-lined with the rose garland design and applied with a transfer print inscribing the event.

1912

Hazledene landscape in a dark green colourway. The same version continued in produced at the Cobridge works.

Cornflower. Redeveloped with brown colourway also in numerous other colourways.

Cobridge Works
William Moorcroft
1913
Powder Blue also known as Blue Porcelain in later years as marketed by Liberty. Other colours also experimented with such as pink and celadon.
Fish. This would seem to be the earliest date that pieces decorated with fish and aquatic plants were first made, in deference to the magnificent Carp designs of the early 1900s. This design was later simplified with different types of fish being drawn in the 1930s when the design was frequently used.
1914
Persian.
1916
Monochrome lustre wares. An usual array of ornamental wares were produced with various solid monochrome brilliant and matte lustre glazes. These wares coincide with the production of monochrome tablewares.
1918
Naturalistic floral wares. During this later period one can find the 'naturalistic' treatment of flowers such as orchids, narcissus, poppies and cornflowers used with a darker colourway producing an altogether more sombre yet exotic feel.
Monochrome ground panelled wares. This group comes in many guises but all have a monochrome coloured ground with quatrefoil panels, bands or other such compartments within which there are floral or fruit designs decorated with polychrome or monochrome colour palettes. Some of the main wares in this section are the powder blue ground wares with scalloped quatrefoil compartments of flowers and foliage.
1919
Flambé technique was introduced at about this time. As Walter commented "he never discovered how or from what source my father acquired the technique of producing flambé".
First Word War Commemorative wares.
1920
Cornflower re-drawn. This version is akin to a rather hard-edged version of the 'naturalistic' wares with overlapping flower heads in strong colours and can be seen in various colourways and on a variety of coloured grounds.
1922
Moonlit Blue landscape.
1923
Big Poppy. With a particularly bulbous flower head.
Eventide landscape.
1926
Dawn landscape.
Black Landscape. This design is very rare with only a few pieces known to exist and even then there are variations in overall design. The origin of the design is a development of the earliest Florian Landscape and Hazledene Landscape with the path receding into the distance and distant bushy topped trees. This design includes numerous birds in flight above the trees. One version has a matte glaze effect and another piece has a brilliant smooth glaze. The trees and ground are coloured in a mottled green and white effect.

1928

Autumn Leaves or Autumn Leaf, latterly also known as Berries and Leaves. Walter comments that "this design was created mainly as a vehicle for flambé".

1930

Weeping Willow Tree. Indicative of the simplification that William applied to new and old designs during the 1930s.

Weeping Beech. Appears in a variety of colours from flambé to 'salt glaze'.

South African Flower – (protea cynaroides).

Fish and Seaweed design. Used to a great extent in the 1930s with variations in the type of fish and marine life, plants, jelly fish, etc that were used. Wares can be found in a few colourways and often covered with a flambé glaze.

Wisteria re-drawn and used on various grounds. Matt plain cream.

Orange and Blossom. Very few piece were made mainly used on tableware or a large jug.

Peacock feather. This design is an extension of the earlier design but reflects the simplification that many patterns underwent during this period. At it's most minimalist this design become just the peacock eye, often in combination with other equally minimalist flower heads. Often found combined with banding as well as table ware sets.

1932

Waratah. Again with a large bulbous flower head as with Big Poppy.

1933

Sunray for tableware. A variation of the powder blue used between 1933 and 1937 advertised in Liberty catalogues.

Green for tableware. Another variation for use on tableware. Other colours were also experimented with such as purple and pale blue much the same as some of the earlier experiments shortly after the Cobridge works opened.

1934

Waving Corn.

1935

Honesty. Simplified design often with banding.

Tulip. Simplified design sometimes found with geometric banding.

George V commemorative wares. Various wares. A commemorative beaker vase was designed by Walter, his first design, whilst he was still at school with William's signature on the base.

Yacht. The ultimate in simplification in Moorcroft terms, utilised on tablewares and ornamental wares.

Freesia. Again often found of darker grounds of blue and blue graduated to yellow. Also combined with other flowers, such as Cornflowers, in a floral spray effect.

1936

Spring Flowers. This continued in production until the late 1950s

Honeysuckle. A rare pattern

Natural ware. This refers to a collection of wares that were made in response to the influence of Studio Pottery consisting of ribbed hand thrown wares, sometimes with a wheel impressed decorative band, in a variety of monochrome colours and/or mottled colours

1937

Tiger Lily. **Walter Moorcroft** design signed by William. Designed after a painting by Walter in 1934 whilst at Rugby school.

Orchids. Later continued by Walter with dramatic results. Continued until 1972.
Edward VIII Commemorative wares.
George VI Commemorative ware.
1938
Anemone. With large open bulbous flowers and elongated foliage.
Wildfowl/Ducks. This appears to be a trial or one-off design that was not put into production and was not designed by Walter Moorcroft, as a comment by him suggests.
Pelican. This appears to be a trial or one-off design that was not put into production and was designed by **Walter Moorcroft** (thanks for an acknowledgement by Walter).
Fighting Cock. Designed by **Walter Moorcroft**. One of Walter's earliest designs although signed by William. Only a few pieces with this design were made each with various colourways.
Poppy. With large and small open poppy heads.
Pelican. Designed by **Walter Moorcroft**. This was designed on a 'natural pottery' vase in pale colours.
Swallow. Designed by **Walter Moorcroft**.
Tiger Lily. Designed by **Walter Moorcroft** but with William's signature. Bought by the Duchess of Gloucester when she visited the British Industries Fair.
African Lily. Designed by William from flower drawings on a menu from the Union Castle line brought over by a South African customer. Later re-used by Walter in the 1950s
Fuchsia. Stems of flowers and foliage. Special commission lamp bases made for Crest Co of Chicago with a yellow flambé glaze
Smoker's accessories designed by T Eaton Co of Canada.
1939
Clematis. Designed by William Moorcroft and extended into a range by Walter from 1946. Later re-drawn by Walter in 1958.

Walter Moorcroft
1947
Tiger Lily vase, 17" (illustrated in *Walter Moorcroft – Memories of Life and Living* page 40) was made following the original watercolour by Walter in 1934 of a pink Tiger Lily.
Columbine. Designed by Walter Moorcroft. First produced on a 7" vase and a footed bowl 4½".
Anemone special vase. Designed by William but most frequently used and associated with Walter.
1949
Hibiscus. Designed by Walter Moorcroft following the arrival of some pressed flowers from Jamaica. This design became a vital part of post war production in Moorcroft's. From about 1960 the whole range was re-drawn to get the right balance of colour between the flower and background which meant omitting the bud at times.
1950
Bougainvillaea. Designed by Walter Moorcroft during the early 1950s having been sent pressed flowers and watercolour sketches from Jamaica in 1949. This designed was apparently produced in a variety of colourways, some specifically to meet requests from retailers.
Walter introduces moulded wares into production with great success. The first piece being an octagonal ashtray decorated with an open Columbine.

1952

Orchid Flambé vase. Designed by Walter Moorcroft. Specifically made for the First Class Deck, Royal Mail Line. SS Andres.

Bourgainvillaea. Designed by Walter Moorcroft. Inspired by pressed flowers sent from Jamaica. Produced in various colourways including flambé.

Tiger Lily Flambé. Two large open flowers in yellow and red on a blue/green ground.

1953

Elizabeth II Commemorative wares. Designed by Walter Moorcroft for the coronation of Queen Elizabeth II, including: a vase (6"), a small bowl each produced in very small quantities but not an official limited edition.

1954

Freesia. Designed by Walter Moorcroft. Initially launched on two vases, a bowl and a coaster. *Turquoise ground introduced. Produced using coloured slip.*

1957

Dianthus. Designed by Walter Moorcroft. Produced on only one shape against a graduated blue/green to grey/green ground in numbers limited to between 50 and 100.

1958

Wild Arum. Designed by Walter Moorcroft. Also known as Arum Lily appears in various forms from the full tall flower with high open flower to just a speckled leaf. Also produced in various colours. Withdrawn in 1985.

Clematis. Designed by Walter Moorcroft. New design by Walter breaking away from his father's style. Used on numerous pieces until 1983. Used with certain colourways and on certain shapes in very limited numbers such as a small turquoise ground vase.

Caribbean. Designed by Walter Moorcroft. Produced as a special commission for the exclusive Trimingham store in Bermuda for a set of tankards. Use of turquoise slip ground.

African Lily. Designed by Walter Moorcroft. Redrawn in the late 1950s

Yellow ground introduced.

New clean lined shapes introduced.

1959

Marine. Designed by Walter Moorcroft. Inspired by drawing of exotic fish by Lis Moorcroft.

Poplar Leaves. Designed by Walter Moorcroft. Produced on only one large spherical vase and in very small numbers with a band of various sized leaves against an ivory, wood smoke and flambé ground.

1960

Hedgevine. Spiralling bands of berries and foliage on a deep blue mottled ground and a white ground. This design was only produced on one shape in two heights (one being a 12" vase) and had a short production run.

Leaves in the Wind. Designed by Walter Moorcroft. Launched at the Blackpool Trade fair with two inverted leaves in tones of yellow and brown on a white ground. Although they initially sold well, there were no reorders. Withdrawn in 1962.

1963

Fuchsia. Design by Walter Moorcroft but only reached the trials stage never going into production. A simple pendent flower with a small bud and two leaves.

1964

Tiger Lily. Variation, on a graduated yellow/green ground with flambé glaze.

Rhododendron vase. Designed by Walter Moorcroft. This was a trial piece on a 7½" bulbous vase, with a large lavish open flower head in tones of red with yellow stamen, leaves either side. Never produced.

Four new miniature shapes introduced initially hand thrown until 1969/70 and then cast.

1965

Tiger Lily plate. Variation. Very limited numbers, possibly only six, were made with a yellow and red detailed Tiger Lily and buds against a yellow ground. These are thought to be trials.

Four moulded ashtray designs.

1967

Poinsettia Christmas plate. Designed by Walter Moorcroft. A special commission by Woodward's, a store in Vancover although not put into production.

Maize vase. Walter Moorcroft design created as a special commission for T. Eaton of Canada as a lamp base but not produced (12"). Produced on a white ground and flambé.

1968

Coral Hibiscus. Designed by Walter Moorcroft. Redrawn Hibiscus design with pink flowers on an olive green and ivory ground. In 1982 and 1983 a dish (10" diameter) and a bulbous vase were produced in a limited edition of 100 pieces for a special order in Canada.

1969

Maple Leaf lamp base. Designed by Walter Moorcroft. A special commission for Eaton's of Canada having sent pressed leaves for Walter.

1970

Pansy Nouveau. Designed by Walter Moorcroft. A special commission for Ebeling and Reuss Moorcroft distributors in the USA. Withdrawn autumn 1972. Flowers in blue and yellow amongst leaves in a band on a pale green ground.

Oval range of shapes introduced at the end of the year. First shown in 1971.

Flambé production came to an end due to the change from coal gas to natural gas and subsequent loss of vital chemical atmosphere.

1971

Alamander. Designed by Walter Moorcroft. Drawn in Bermuda and produced in very limited numbers on a small oblong box with a pale yellow flower on a green ground.

Bermuda Lily. Designed by Walter Moorcroft. Developed in Bermuda whilst on a business trip and produced on a variety on colourways. Initial experimental pieces on a turquoise ground before settling on the olive green ground.

Orchid. 'Laelia Autumnalis' version of a large open flower. Taken from a Yearbook of the Royal Horticultural Society.

1972

Bermuda Lily. Designed by Walter Moorcroft. White flower on an olive green ground

1975

Eastern Lily. Designed by Walter Moorcroft. A development of the Bermuda Lily design following a request from Canada for Bermuda Lily on an ivory ground which was not practical.

1976

Magnolia. Designed by Walter Moorcroft. Withdrawn at the end of 1999.

The Moorcroft Trophy. Designed by Walter Moorcroft as a one off piece for the Association of Golf Club Secretaries.

1977

Silver Jubilee Commemorative Plate. Designed by Walter Moorcroft for Silver Jubilee of Queen Elizabeth II produced in a limited edition of 125 pieces (8½" diameter).

1978

Jungle Brown Lily. Designed by Walter Moorcroft. Variation of the Bermuda Lily design with a yellow flower on a deep brown ground.

Cigarette lighter designed and formed part of a new smoker's set. This set was sold in satin lined blue boxes, the first appearance of the Moorcroft boxes.

1979

Hibiscus dish. Designed by Walter Moorcroft and inscribed Best Wishes. Made especially for Ted Takarada of Yokohama, Japan.

1980

Wild Rose. Designed by Walter Moorcroft. Commission by Liberty for the launch of the Mini Metro car/vehicle. Produced only as prototypes with two open flowers and a bud amongst leaves on a wood smoke, pale blue and pale yellow grounds.

1982

Anemone Year Plate. Designed by Walter Moorcroft. Produced in a limited edition of 200 on a blue ground (8½" diameter).

New range of boxes and small dishes introduced, included 110 items in all, decorated with standard designs and different background colours. The diamond and clover shapes withdrawn in 1984/85.

1983

Hibiscus Year Plate. Designed by Walter Moorcroft. Limited edition 250 (8½").

Hibiscus Year Bell. Designed by Walter Moorcroft. Limited edition 200 each but only perhaps only 100 or less of each were made.

Jungle Brown Lily vase. Initially designed by Walter Moorcroft in 1978.

1984

Columbine Year Plate. Designed by Walter Moorcroft. Limited edition of 250 (8½").

Columbine Year Bell. Designed by Walter Moorcroft. Limited edition of 200 but only perhaps only 100 or less of each were made.

Butterfly Bramble vase. Designed by Walter Moorcroft.

Butterfly Bluebell vase. Designed by Walter Moorcroft.

Wild Arum vase. Designed by Walter Moorcroft.

1985

Walter Moorcroft Commemorative Plate. Designed by the staff to commemorate Walter's 50 years at the factory.

Anemone Year Plate. Designed by Walter Moorcroft. Limited edition of 250 on a white ground (8½").

Anemone Year Bell. Designed by Walter Moorcroft. Limited edition of 100.

Marston Brewery (Burton-on-Trent) Jug and ashtray. Some 500 pieces of each were made.

Campanula. Designed by Walter Moorcroft. In 1984 the prototypes of small five petalled blue flowers, were tube-lined. These were then used to make moulded versions at a much reduced cost.

Thistle. Designed by Walter Moorcroft. Produced for Churchill China and made using moulds.

Bluebell. Designed by Walter Moorcroft. Produced for Churchill China and made using moulds.

Daffodil. Designed by Walter Moorcroft. Produced for Churchill China and made using moulds.

Geranium. Designed by Walter Moorcroft. Sketched by the swimming pool in Crete. Engraved in the mould to reduced costs.

Tulip. Walter Moorcroft design. Later Walter reproduced the design using a white flower on an olive green ground produced in a limited edition on a 10" plate, a 7" vase and a 10" plate.

Hibiscus. After a designed by Walter Moorcroft and produced in a new blue colourway by Churchills, without Walter's knowledge. Withdrawn in 1988.

1986

Coral Hibiscus Year Plate. Designed by Walter Moorcroft. Limited edition of 250 (8½").

Coral Hibiscus Year Bell. Designed by Walter Moorcroft. Limited edition of 200 only 100 or less made.

Wild Arum vase. Walter Moorcroft design in a limited edition of 50 (7").

Pineapple Plant vase and planter. Walter design in a limited edition of 100 each (vase 14½").

Chestnut Leaves collection. Walter Moorcroft design produced with a brown or ivory ground on two vases (12" & 14½") and a tray (9" long). All made in limited editions of 50.

Magnolia. Special edition of 20 olive green ground vases (12") after original design from 1975.

Bottle Oven mug. Designed by Walter Moorcroft. Produced for the Bottle Oven Museum & Shop in connection with the First National Garden Festival, Stoke-on-Trent.

Tulip collection. Walter Moorcroft design re-issued on an olive green ground in a limited edition of 50 pieces including two vases (10" & 7") and a 10" plate. Also produced for sale in Canada with a yellow tulips on a blue ground and pink tulips on a blue ground again using the same shapes in a limited edition of 50 pieces.

Maize. Walter Moorcroft design. Original design created in 1967 as a special commission for T. Eaton of Canada and re-introduced in a limited edition of 100 vases (12").

Fruit & Vine collection. **Designed by Marjorie Kubanda.** A band of Grapes and apples alternating with leaves on deep blue ground on a planter in a limited edition of 500. A vase was sold in Australia and Canada and was made into an exclusive lamp base for Liberty's with a green ground.

Sally Tuffin
1987

Freesias Walter Moorcroft plate. A special one off design by the staff of Moorcroft on Walter's retirement in February (14"). Inscribed "1935-1987. Walter Moorcroft."

Freesias Year Plate – **Designed by Walter Moorcroft**. Produced in a limited edition of 250 (8½").

Dragon collection. **Designed by Trevor Critchlow** as a one off design.

Ivy. Designed by Wendy Mason and Julie Dolan produced on a vase (7") and a bowl, Withdrawn in the same year.

Fairy Rings collection. **Designed by Philip Richardson**, Withdrawn 1990.

Honeycomb collection. **Designed by Philip Richardson** on six shapes with bees in flight amongst a honeycomb. Withdrawn in 1989.

Reeds at Sunset collection. **Designed by Philip Richardson** on six shapes. Withdrawn in 1990.

Moorcroft vase. Design by Sally Tuffin. This globular vase (6½") produced in several different colourways.

Rose collection. Design by Sally Tuffin on a limited range of wares but with various colourways until 1988 when only a red rose was used. Withdrawn in 1991.

Violet collection. Designed by Sally Tuffin. Withdrawn at the end of 1999, one of Sally Tuffin's last two designs.

Banksia collection. Designed by Sally Tuffin initially on a mottled blue/green ground and later a graduated green ground. Produced on five pieces mainly for sale in Australia. Withdrawn 1990.

Thaxted Men mug. **Arranged by Walter Moorcroft.** A special commission for the annual Morris Dancing Festival.

Magnolia mug. **Designed by Walter Moorcroft** as a special commission for Liberty's and later put on general release. The first in a series of such mug commissions.

1988

Cockerel Year plate. Designed by Sally Tuffin. Produced in a limited edition of 250 (8").

Wattle collection. Designed by Sally Tuffin for sale in Australian. At least eight pieces in the range with pendulous circular yellow flowers. Withdrawn in 1990.

Plum collection. Designed by Sally Tuffin. Birds perched amongst fruit laden branches, withdrawn 1990.

Lemon collection. Designed by Sally Tuffin. Produced on large pieces, decorated with birds perched on branches laden with lemons. Withdrawn 1990.

Grapevine vase. Designed by Sally Tuffin. A special piece available only to members of the Designed in 1987 and available only in 1988.

Sunflower range. Designed by Sally Tuffin. The tallest a 27" vase.

Peacock range. Designed by Sally Tuffin. Designed by Liberty's. Withdrawn 1990.

First Fleet. Designed by Sally Tuffin. Originally produced for the Australian bicentenary but later put on general realise in limited numbers. A covered jar was produced in a limited edition of 25, a charger and a vase (14") in an edition of 100 (Australia) and another 150 for general release.

Lion's Den vase. Designed by Sally Tuffin. A special commission made in a limited edition of 50 for the retailer Lion's Den (10").

Eagle Owl vase. Designed by Sally Tuffin. Limited edition of 500 (112").

Polar Bear vase. Designed by Sally Tuffin. Globular vase produced in a limited edition of 250 for sale in Canada (6½").

Dinosaur vase. Designed by Sally Tuffin. A special piece made for sale in North America in a limited edition of 300 (9½").

Saki cups. Designed by Sally Tuffin. A special commission for the Ato Galleries in Tokyo, produced in a limited edition of 500 sets (2" high).

Robin collection. Designed by Sally Tuffin. Produced on a limited number of pieces, including a mug, and withdrawn in 1991, only to be reintroduced on a blue ground and withdrawn again in 1992.

Hot Air Balloon plate. Designed by Sally Tuffin. A special commission for R & R Collectibles produced in a limited edition of 200 (14").

Heron. Designed by Philip Richardson on a large vase (27") and a charger. This was a variation of the Reeds at Sunset with the addition of a heron.

Plumb mug. Designed by Sally Tuffin as a special commission for Liberty's.

1989

Fish Year plate. Designed by Sally Tuffin. Produced in a limited edition of 250 (8").

Anemone range. **Walter Moorcroft's latest design** in the continuation of the Anemone wares. Produced on yellow, green and blue ground, the yellow and green ground being withdrawn in 1991. The blue ground range which appears on 22 shapes and by 1998 on 10 lamp bases, was withdrawn at the end of 1999.

Anemone. **Designed by Walter Moorcroft**. Redrawn.

Fruit & Vine collection. **Designed by Marjorie Kubanda**. The pattern as above produced in a limited edition of 75 on a plate (8") for the retailer Showplace of Melbourne, Australia. 50 other plates were also made without the Showpiece mark.

Thaxted Guildhall plate. Designed by Sally Tuffin. A special commission for the Trustees of Thaxted Guildhall, the first in a series of three, produced in a limited edition of 500 (8").

Daisy vase. Designed by Sally Tuffin. A special piece only available to members of the MCC for the year (7").

Finches range. Designed by Sally Tuffin. Initially designed on a large 27" vase and then extended onto a wide range of shapes using a blue ground, over a celadon body, and then from 1989 an ochre ground (withdrawn 1990). Withdrawn at the end of 1996. The same design appeared in 1991 on a green ground also on a new tea set (withdrawn 1992) and on a new teal green ground in 1993.

Tulip range. Designed by Sally Tuffin. Red tulips produced on a number of shapes. Later produced with a black tulip and re-worked colourway.

Golden Lily vase. Designed by Sally Tuffin after fabric design by J H Dearle for William Morris. Produced in blue ground and on white (12"). Later additions.

Orange vase. Designed by Sally Tuffin. A bird perched on a branch laden with oranges on a white ground (10"). Withdrawn 1990.

Elephant vase. Designed by Sally Tuffin. A special centenary commission for Thomas Goode depicting the Minton modelled elephants for their showroom. The two handled vases made in a limited edition of 25 (13").

Penguin collection. Designed by Sally Tuffin. Three different designs used on 10" plates and another design on a vase each produced in a limited edition, 350 vases and 150 of each plate.

Blackberry mug. Designed by Sally Tuffin as a special commission for Liberty's.

Beaufort House mug. Designed by Sally Tuffin. A special commission for Richards Butler.

Museum mug. Designed by Sally Tuffin. A special piece made to commemorate the opening of the Moorcroft Museum.

1990

Buttercup Year plate. Designed by Sally Tuffin. Made in an edition of 250 (8").

Rose jug. Designed by Sally Tuffin. A special available only to members of the MCC for the year.

Pohutukawa vase. Designed by Sally Tuffin. A special commission for Tanfield Pottery of Auckland, New Zealand, in a limited edition of 100 (5"). In 1992 an edition of 220 plates (8") were also commissioned.

Spring Blossom range. Designed by Sally Tuffin. Produced on a number of shapes including a mug and withdrawn in 1991.

Vine plate. Designed by Sally Tuffin. A special commission for Selfridges, London, in a limited edition of 50 (10").

Swan. Designed by Sally Tuffin. The globular vase and a 10" plate produced in a limited edition of 350 pieces each.

Temptation. Designed by Sally Tuffin. Produced with apples amongst spring blossom in a limited edition of 500 on a bowl (10½").

Carp collection. Designed by Sally Tuffin. Initially produced on a two-handled vase and later on other vases and plates using a celadon body in 1991. Withdrawn at the end of 1996.

Rose Hip mug. Designed by Sally Tuffin as a special commission for Liberty's.

Peter the Pig. Modelled by Roger Mitchell after the Wemyss Pottery original from the early twentieth century and decorated with Sally Tuffin's Temptation design.

1991

Tudor Rose Year plate. Designed by Sally Tuffin. Produced in a limited edition of 500 (8"). The same design was also produced in a limited edition of 100 pieces in a different colourway.

Sweet pea vase. Designed by Sally Tuffin. A special piece only available to MCC Members (10").

Bottle Kiln mugs. Designed by Sally Tuffin. A special piece only available to members attending the Collector Club weekend.

Spitalfields Market. Designed by Sally Tuffin. A special commemorative plate (8") to celebrate the move of Spitalfields Market to the new site at Temple Mills after 300 years. Produced in a limited edition of 500. A plate was presented to HRH the Duke of Gloucester during the opening of Temple Mills.

Green Finch vase. Designed by Sally Tuffin. A Special Events piece for the year.

Gothic Windows vase. Designed by Sally Tuffin. A special design sold exclusively at the Collectors Showcase in London and produced in a limited edition of 100 pieces in two colourways (5").

Midsummer Night's Dream ginger jar. Designed by Sally Tuffin. A special commission for the specialist Moorcroft retailers B & W Thornton, Stratford-on-Avon. The first in a series of such commissions, this one in a limited edition of 250 pieces.

Abbots Bromley Chalice. Special commission for the Thaxted Morris Men to commemorate 50 years of dancing in 'The Morris Ring' (10").

John Webb's Windmill plate. Designed by Sally Tuffin. A special commission for the Trustees of Thaxted Guildhall, the second in a series of three, produced in a limited edition of 500 (8").

Dandelion vase. Designed by Sally Tuffin. A special commission by Neville Pundole, Norfolk, produced in a limited edition of 250 pieces (5"). An 8" vase was also produced in 1992 again for Neville Pundole in an edition of 200 pieces.

Carp vase. Designed by Sally Tuffin. Produced in a limited edition of 100 on the 28" vase.

Golden Lily charger. Designed by Sally Tuffin as an addition to previous wares on both a blue and a white ground.

Bramble range. Designed by Sally Tuffin. Over the years the range was extended to include over 20 shapes including a tea set as well as being used on a new 11" vase in 1993. One of Sally Tuffin's last two designs to be withdrawn end of 1999.

Buttercup range. Designed by Sally Tuffin. An extension of the 1990 Yearplate. Also made into a tea set along with Bramble, violet and green finch.

Toadstool. **Designed by Philip Richardson**, this was a re-working of the Fairy Rings design in a different colourway. Withdrawn in the same year.

Purple Magnolia. **Designed by Walter Moorcroft.** The 1970s Purple Magnolia design is given a new wine colourway and re-leased. Initially produced exclusively for the Australian market for 1991 and then for general release in the following year.

1992

Passion Flower Year plate. **Designed by Sally Tuffin**. Produced in a limited edition of 500 (8").

Autumn Flowers vase. **Designed by Sally Tuffin** after a William Morris design (12").

Bottle Kiln mugs. **Designed by Sally Tuffin**. A special piece only available to members attending the Collector Club weekend.

Nasturtium ginger jar. **Designed by Sally Tuffin**. A special only available to members of the MCC for the year.

Ophelia ginger jar. **Designed by Sally Tuffin**. A special commission for the specialist Moorcroft retailers B & W Thornton, Stratford-on-Avon. Part of a series of such commissions, this one in a limited edition of 250 pieces.

Sultan's Palace vase. **Designed by Sally Tuffin**. A special commission to commemorate the Silver Jubilee of the reign of His Majesty Duli Yang Maha Mulia Paduka Seri Baginda Sultan Haji Hassanal Bolkiah Mu'zzaddin Waddaulah. Limited edition of 65 (8").

Mamoura range. **Designed by Sally Tuffin**. The first of various landscape designs.

Cluny range. **Designed by Sally Tuffin**. Landscape design influenced by the medieval tapestries at Cluny. The range was extended to at least twelve shapes with 2 lamp bases. Withdrawn at the end of 1998 when 2 more lamp bases having been added to the range.

Rain Forrest range. **Designed by Sally Tuffin**. Produced with various flowers in different pieces. The range was extended in 1993. A limited edition of 150 vases (16½") were produced in the same year. In 1993 a special commission of 100 7" vases were made for Michael & Kate Trim with profits donated to the rain forest, as with the 16½" vase.

Lattice collection. **Designed by Sally Tuffin**.

Seasons collection. **Designed by Sally Tuffin**. The seasons represented by different colourways.

Cat plate. **Designed by Sally Tuffin**. A special design for Richard Dennis, London, in a limited of 300 (10").

Rachel Bishop
1993

Dove Year plate. Designed by Sally Tuffin. Produced in a limited edition of 500 (8").

Blue Gum .Designed by Sally Tuffin. Two vases produced for sale in Australia, a 7" vase in an edition of 500 and a 16½" vase in an edition of 50 pieces.

Roses. Designed by Sally Tuffin. A box and cover and a vase (10") with blue, pink and yellow roses following the 1990 design produced in a limited edition of 500.

Windsor Carnation vase. Designed by Sally Tuffin. A special commission for Talents of Windsor in a limited edition of 300 (11").

Tigris vase. Designed by Rachel Bishop. This shown at the NEC Spring Fair in Birmingham, February 1993. The limited edition of 150 vases was sold out by the June, 16" high.

The Winter's Tale. Designed by Rachel Bishop. Commission for B & W Thornton of Stratford upon Avon, 6" high.

Fuchsia vase. Designed by Rachel Bishop. MCC vase for 1993. Innovative use of red tube-lining and unpainted areas within the design, 6" high.

Oberon charger. Designed by Rachel Bishop. Special commission for the retirement of John Rainford of the Richards Butler law firm. 14" diameter.

White Rose vase. Designed by Rachel Bishop. Special occasions, 5" high.

Butterfly vase. Designed by Rachel Bishop. Specifically designed for the MCC Open Day, 5" high. Limited numbered edition. There was a residue of 125 unnumbered pieces.

Pansy range. Designed by Rachel Bishop. Launched in July 1993 this range was produced on some 14 pieces as well as six lamp bases. Withdrawn at the end of 1998.

1994

Kyoto vase. Designed by Rachel Bishop. Shown at the NEC Spring Fair July 1994 (24" high).

William Morris Golden Lily range. Designed by Rachel Bishop. Two colourways both discontinued in 1995 with the exception of the 10" ivory vase.

Oberon range. Designed by Rachel Bishop. Nineteen pieces in the range to start with, extended to 24 by 1998 with some 13 lamp bases. In 1999 the range was altered again with the addition of new shapes whilst others were retired leaving 23 pieces in the range, lamp base were reduced to 11.

Butterfly range. Designed by Rachel Bishop. Produced on 13 pieces as well as six lamp bases. Withdrawn at the end of 1997.

Foxgloves range. Designed by Rachel Bishop. By 1998 this range was produced on 10 pieces and six lamp bases. Withdrawn at the end of 1998.

Hypericum range. Designed by Rachel Bishop. Withdrawn 1995.

Peacock Year plate. Designed by Rachel Bishop.

Trellis Clock. Designed by Rachel Bishop. Limited edition of 250 pieces.

Heartsease Special Occasions vase. Designed by Rachel Bishop. Sold just under 1000 pieces, 5" high.

Snowdrop two handled loving cup. Designed by Rachel Bishop. MCC piece, 6" high. In all 525 'perfect' vases were produced which does not include the numerous 'almost perfect' pieces. (Limited to one piece per member)

Adonis vase. Designed by Rachel Bishop. A special for the MCC Open Day also known as the 'Pheasants Eye', 6" high.

Bee Coaster. Designed by Rachel Bishop. One off special for the MCC Day for collectors to have personal messages inscribed.

Inca range. Designed by Rachel Bishop. Initially 17 pieces in the range. Withdrawn at the end of 1996.

King Lear ginger jar. Designed by Rachel Bishop. A special commission for B & W Thornton, the four in the series, 6" high.

Kyoto range. Designed by Rachel Bishop. Developed onto five pieces and withdrawn at the end of 1996.

1995

Lamia vase. Designed by Rachel Bishop. Limited edition centre piece for the NEC International Spring Fair.

Daffodil vase. Designed by Rachel Bishop. Limited edition of 250 pieces, 14" high.

England vase. Designed by Rachel Bishop. Limited edition, 9" high.

Cockatoo Vase & Plate. Designed by Rachel Bishop. The plate, 10", produced in a limited edition of 350 pieces and the vase, 10", made in an edition of only 60 pieces.

Squirrel Year Plate. Designed by Rachel Bishop. 8" diameter.

Summer Lawn vase. Designed by Rachel Bishop. The special occasions vase which sold 520 pieces in the year.

Morello Bowl. Designed by Rachel Bishop. MCC oval bowl, 9" long.

Malahide. Designed by Rachel Bishop. A special commission for the retailer James Macintyre & Co, Leeds 5" high.

Cymbeline ginger jar. Designed by Rachel Bishop. A special commission for B & W Thornton. This was the fifth and last design in the series, 6" high.

Hellebore vase. Designed by Rachel Bishop. Special for the MCC Open Day, all 160 pieces sold during the weekend of Open Day, 5" high.

Fruit mugs. Designed by Rachel Bishop. Made to be sold in the Moorcroft factory shop.

MCC mugs. Designed by Rachel Bishop. Special for the Moorcroft Collectors' Club members. Only 60 pieces were made at the end of the day.

Love in a Mist. Designed by Rachel Bishop. The vase was produced initially in a limited edition 200, then increased to 300. The jardiniere and stand limited to 50 pieces.

Mackintosh range. Designed by Rachel Bishop. Launched September Birmingham Trade Fair. In the January Earls court Lighting show the Mackintosh lamp (14") won the Gold Award for Excellence, Rachel Bishop having specifically designed shades for the lamp bases. By 1997, there were 12 pieces in the range and five lamp bases. In 1998 two new lamp bases were added and in 1999 an 8" and an 9½" vase were added.

Ponga Fern. Designed by Rachel Bishop. Vase commissioned by Tanfield Potter in a limited edition of 150 pieces and used as part of a New Zealand promotion.

1996

Morning Glory year plate. Designed by Rachel Bishop. 8" diameter.

Golden Lily Ivory collection. Designed by Rachel Bishop. Produced on four pieces, three vases and a tray, as well as a lamp base. Withdrawn end of 1997.

Leicester collection. Designed by Rachel Bishop. Produced on three vases and a coaster as well as a lamp base. Withdrawn at the end of 1997.

Snakeshead collection. Designed by Rachel Bishop. Produced on three vases and a tray as well as lamp base. Withdrawn at the end of 1997.

Strawberry Thief collection. Designed by Rachel Bishop. Produced on two vases, a coaster and a bowl and cover as well as a lamp base. Withdrawn at the end of 1997.

Tree Bark Thief. Designed by Rachel Bishop. A massive jardiniere and stand limited to 50. Vase (14" high)

Noah's Ark ginger jar. Designed by Rachel Bishop. A special for MCC members (6"). By the end of the year over 1,000 pieces has been sold making it the most successful MCC piece so far. Limited to one piece per member.

Lamia range. Designed by Rachel Bishop. Produced on 22 pieces initially as well as ten lamp bases. By 1999 the range was amended with the withdrawal of some shapes and the addition of new ones leaving 21 pieces in the range, the 7" lamp base was lost but two others, a 6" and an 8" were added.

Bryony vase. Designed by Rachel Bishop. Special occasions vase (5" high).

Convolvulus mug. Designed by Rachel Bishop. A special Open Day piece

A pair of **Phoenix in an Oak Forest vases** – Designed by Rachel Bishop. Retirement form Richards Butler. November 1996 (24"). For the first time Sgraffito was used on the tree trunks.

1997

Yacht vase. Designed by Rachel Bishop with technical assistance from Justin Emery (works manager) after an original design by William Moorcroft. Produced for 1997 Centenary. Some coloured versions were auctioned at the Centenary Open Weekend. Some 3,000 vases were ordered although huge production problems entailing the glaze continually dripping during firing lead to the suspension of production until a solution was found. Suspension was supposed to have been lifted by 31 January 1999. As a consequence a great many 'almost' prefect' pieces have been sold in the factory shop.

Phoenix range. Designed by Rachel Bishop. 9 pieces in all introduced together with 4 lamp bases. The Phoenix lamp base (11") won a silver Excellence Award at the Earls Court Lighting Show. Withdrawn at the end of 1998.

Poppy range. Designed by Rachel Bishop. Designed in 1995 but held back until the Centenary year the range was launched with on 20 pieces together with eight lamp bases. This also included a massive 27" vase. The range was reduced to 13 pieces and six lamp bases in 1999. Withdrawn at the end of 1999.

After the Storm. **Designed by Walter Moorcroft** specifically for the Moorcroft Centenary. Produced in a limited edition of 200 pieces (20" high). A few trial vases (10") were sold during the weekend of the Centennial Dinner in October in the shop.

Carousel numbered editions. Designed by Rachel Bishop. This edition consisted of five pieces including two new shapes, a 6" ginger jar and a 5" vase. All the pieces were made following orders placed within the year. Use of blue tube-lining on three of the pieces particularly on the passion flowers and raspberry flowers. Something in the region of 1,200 ginger jars were made in total.

Iris jug. Designed by Rachel Bishop. Available only to members of the MCC with one piece per member (8" high). 1,570 jugs were sold making it the most successful Club piece to date.

Frog charger. Designed by Rachel Bishop. A special one-off presentation piece for Gill Moorcroft's 25 years with Moorcroft.

Frog coaster. Designed by Rachel Bishop.

The Centennial plate. Designed by Rachel Bishop. Depicting the Moorcroft bottle kiln. Made in a limited edition of 750 pieces (10").

Rough Hawk's Beard vase. Designed by Rachel Bishop. A special occasions piece accompanying John Moorcroft on his visits (5"). The last Special Occasions piece before the new Collectors' Day pieces.

Tansy vase. Designed by Rachel Bishop. Open Weekend piece (6").

Rudbeckia vase. Designed by Rachel Bishop. A special Open Weekend piece (8"). An experimental vase sold for £420 in the October Centennial Auction.

Spring Flowers mug. Designed by Rachel Bishop.

Thaxted Parish Church. Designed by Rachel Bishop. The third in a series of plates commissioned by the Thaxted Guildhall (8").

Phoenix Bird vase. Designed by Rachel Bishop. A special promotions piece (8") available only during book promotions (*Moorcroft – The Phoenix Years* by Fraser Street).

Sea Horse plate. Designed by Jeanne McDougall (10") sold during the weekend of the Centennial Dinner in October in the shop. This would appear to be a early offering of what was launched as Martinique in 1998. Pieces were also sold at the Centennial auctions.

Coral Reef Fish vase. Designed by Jeanne McDougall sold during the weekend of the Centennial Dinner in October in the shop. Twenty such vases formed the winning prizes for both nights of the quiz during the same weekend. Apparently, only 35 vases were made in total. This would appear to be an early version of the Martinique numbered edition launched in 1998. A variety of trials in differing colourways were sold in the shop during the 11-12 October weekend.

Anemone vase. Designed by Walter Moorcroft in a red colourway. Sold during the weekend of the Centennial Dinner in October in the shop.

Autumnal Poppy vase. Designed by Rachel Bishop. Sold during the weekend of the Centennial Dinner in October in the shop.

Flambé Trials. Several trial pieces of flambé produced by Robert Watson and Justin Emery (consultant) were sold during the weekend of the Centennial Dinner in October in the shop.

Hoya vase. Designed by Rachel Bishop. Two of only 30 vases made for the Australian market was sold during the Centennial Diner auction.

The Design Team
Fish lamp base. Designed by the Design Studio. This experimental design sold for £680 during the two Centennial Dinner auction events in October.
Tiger Lily coaster. Designed by Rachel Bishop. Presented as a gift to each guest at the Centennial dinner with the inscription 1897–1997. The coaster came in three different colourways. A few pieces were later sold in the January sale, 1998, for £55 with seconds pieces selling or £49.50.
An Art Nouveau vase. Designed by the Design Studio (10") was sold for £600 at the Centennial Dinner.

1998
Summers End Year plate. Designed by Rachel Bishop. Produced in a limited edition of 750 (8"). Such pieces would have impressed numbers in the base.
Spike vase. Designed by Rachel Bishop. In all some 400 vases were sold.
Ryden Lane. Designed by Rachel Bishop. Produced in a limited edition of 100 pieces (27"). Trials were sold at the MCC Christmas Weekend.
Maypole. Designed by Wendy Mason on a green ground and on ivory ground (14"). Each produced in a limited edition of 150.
Swallows. Designed by Rachel Bishop and produced in a limited edition of 500 (10").
Royal Tribute. Designed by Rachel Bishop and produced in a limited edition of 400 (10").
Crown Imperial. Designed by Rachel Bishop and produced in a limited edition of 600 (12").
Martinique. Designed by the Jeanne McDougall. Produced on a trumpet shaped vase (12"), a tapering cylindrical vase and a shouldered vase (6") as a numbered edition for the one year only.
Amazon Twilight. Designed by Nicola Slaney on an 8" vase in a numbered edition for one year only.
Victoriana. Designed by Emma Bossons. MCC piece available only to Members of the club, one piece per member. The cut off date was shortened to 31st December 1998, therefore restricting the number of pieces made.
Rockpool. Designed by Wendy Mason on a vase (8") and a bowl (10") in a numbered edition until the end of the year.
Flame of the Forest. Designed by Philip Gibson. Produced on four pieces and three lamp bases. In 1999, the design was extended onto seven pieces.
Puffins. Designed by Carol Lovett. Produced on three vases and two lamp bases initially, extended to 16 pieces in 1999 as well as five lamp bases.
Andalucia. Designed by Beverley Wilkes. Produced on two similar shapes vases (8" and 11") and two lamp bases. Withdrawn at the end of 1999.
Sweet Briar collection. Designed by Rachel Bishop. Produced in pink and yellow colourways on three shapes and one lamp base for each colourway. Altered in 1999 with only the 6" vase carried over to join five new shapes including a clock and three new lamp bases. Withdrawn at the end of 1999.
Passion Fruit range. Designed by Rachel Bishop. Produced on 14 shapes and six lamp bases. Withdrawn at the end of the year after many more 'almost perfects' were produced than 'perfects'. (Should make prices interesting in the future!!)
Furzey Hill. Designed by Rachel Bishop. Produced on four vases and three lamp bases.

Withdrawn at the end of 1999.

Knightwood. Designed by Rachel Bishop. Produced on four vases and three lamp bases. Withdrawn at the end of 1999.

Vereley. Designed by Rachel Bishop. Produced on four vases and three lamp bases. Withdrawn at the end of 1999.

Holly Hatch. Designed by Rachel Bishop. Produced on four vases and three lamp bases. Withdrawn at the end of 1999.

Hawthorn. Designed by Nicola Slaney. Produced as a special limited edition of 400 pieces for Liberty and launched in September (8" high).

A pair of Florian ware vases. From an original design by William Moorcroft presented to **John Moorcroft on his sixtieth birthday** 29 March.

Convolvulus vase. Designed by Debbie Hancock. Produced for the Collector's Club Open Weekend.

Underwood vase. Designed by Debbie Hancock. A special limited edition made for James Macintyre & Co Ltd, Leeds, in 350 pieces (7"). Launched at the retailers on 31 October.

Elegy vase. Designed by Anji Davenport. The full title being 'Elegy in a Country Church Yard' this was a special commission for B & W Thornton in a limited edition of 350 pieces (10").

Swamp Hen ginger jar. Designed by Nicola Slaney as a limited edition of 50 specifically for the MCC Christmas Weekend, 27-28 November.

Orchid vase. Designed by Nicola Slaney as a limited edition of 100 specifically for the Collectors Club Christmas Weekend, 27-28 November.

Indian Summer vase. Designed by Nicola Slaney as a limited edition of 50 specifically for the MCC Christmas Weekend, 27-28 November.

Carnations jug. Designed by Emma Bossons. Produced as a numbered edition specifically for the MCC Christmas Weekend, 27-28 November. 42 jugs and two coasters were sold.

Samburu Giraffe vase. Designed by Anji Davenport in two versions, Dusk and Day produced in a numbered edition of 71.

Hummingbirds. Designed by Anji Davenport. Trials sold at the Christmas Weekend in various colourways (4"). There were also four numbered pieces with the Hibiscus flower and 17 with the Mexican Love Flower.

Malva. Designed by Shirley Hayes. Sold 30 numbered pieces at the MCC Christmas Weekend in various colourways.

Camellia vase. Designed by Debbie Hancock. Various colourways sold at the MCC Christmas Weekend, as well as 33 numbered editions (8").

Christmas Rose. Designed by Nicola Slaney. Produced as a numbered edition and sold at the MCC Christmas Weekend. The vase (7") sold 20 pieces and the coaster (6") nine pieces. Some 52 plates had been made in all.

Mandeville vase. Designed by Anji Davenport. 18 pieces produced as numbered editions and sold at the MCC Christmas Weekend (4").

1999

King Protea vase. Designed by Emma Bossons. Produce in a limited edition of 100 (15").

Tahiti vase. Designed by Nicola Slaney. A numbered piece only available for the year (8").

Aotearoa vase. Designed by Emma Bossons. A numbered piece only available for the year (12").

Kiribati vase. Designed by Emma Bossons. A numbered piece only available for the year (8").

Rarotonga vase. Designed by Emma Bossons. A numbered piece only available for the year (4").

Fiji vase. Designed by Emma Bossons. A numbered piece only available for the year (8").

Birth of Light Millennium Year plate. Designed by Nicola Slaney and painted by Wendy Mason. Produced in a limited edition of 2000 (8").

Serviceberry vase. Designed by Nicola Slaney. Specifically produced for Collectors' Days on a 5" vase and only available at these specific promotions.

Spiraxia. Designed by Emma Bossons. Produced on a vase (11") in a limited edition of 300 and a numbered edition plate (6").

Tiger Lily Year plate. Designed by Nicola Slaney. Produced in a limited edition of 750 pieces (8").

Squirrels vase. Designed by Anji Davenport. Produced in a limited edition of 300 (11").

Balloons collection. Designed by Jeanne McDougall. Produced on seven pieces and three lamp bases, this design features the number "99" on one of the balloons with the possibility that "00" might appear in the future.

California. Designed by Jeanne McDougall. Produced on a vase and as a lamp base (8").

Arizona. Designed by Jeanne McDougall. Produced on a vase as well as a lamp base (9").

Florida. Designed by Jeanne McDougall. Produced as a ginger jar (8").

Gustavia Augusta. Designed by Debbie Hancock. Produced on four pieces and two lamp bases.

Islay. Designed by Rachel Bishop. Produced on four vases and repeated as lamp bases.

Trout range. Designed by Philip Gibson. Produced on 13 pieces as well as five lamp bases. Trial pieces were sold at the Open Weekend.

Meknes vase. Designed by Beverley Wilkes. A special commission for the Guild of Specialist China & Glass Retailers in a limited edition of 350.

Castle Garden. Designed by Debbie Handcock as a special for Talents of Windsor (3") in a limited edition of 500. Launched on 13 November and attended by the designer to sign pieces sold on the day of the launch.

Wisteria vase. Designed by Philip Gibson. Produced for members of the MCC (6").

Floral Garden. Designed by Debbie Hancock. Given to overseas Club members at the Open Weekend in May.

Samarkand Lily vase. Designed by Debbie Hancock as the Open Weekend special piece for Club members. Limited edition of 250.

Woodside Farm tile panel. Designed by Anji Davenport. Available at the Open Weekend.

Indian Summer. Designed by Nicola Slaney. Trial plate sold at the Open Weekend.

For the first time members of the Design Studio created pieces exclusively for the Open Weekend in May. These were all very limited pieces :

Astor. Designed by Debbie Hancock. 43 pieces made.

Colorado. Designed by Debbie Hancock. 38 pieces.

Cape Gooseberry. Designed by Anji Davenport. 34 pieces made.

Oxalis. Designed by Shirley Hayes. 25 pieces made.

Protea. Designed by Emma Bossons. 37 pieces made.
White Holly. Designed by Nicola Slaney. 68 pieces made.
Lavenham vase. Designed by Jeanne McDougall. 17 piece made.
Lavenham coaster. Designed by Jeanne McDougall. 35 pieces.
Melos. Designed by Rachel Bishop. 36 pieces made.
Monkswood. Designed by Philip Gibson. Three pieces made.
Cathedral vase. Designed by Rachel Bishop. First shown in the Milestone' exhibition arranged in the Moorcroft Museum during the 1999 Christmas Weekend.

Jerusalem vase. Designed by Nicola Slaney. Took six months to create.
Rock of Ages. **Designed by Walter Moorcroft**. Three pieces, a limited edition vase (14") of 50 pieces, a limited edition vase (7") 100 pieces and a numbered edition of a plate (6") with orders for the plate finishing on 30 November 1999. The 14" vase was signed by Walter with the other pieces being initialled by him. These pieces were only available from November with some trial pieces appearing at the Christmas Club Weekend (MCCCW).
Purple Aquilegia jug. Designed by Philip Gibson specifically for sale through Antiques Lifestyle magazine (9"). This was produced in a limited edition of 250.
Astrantia vase. Designed by Shirley Hayes. Produced exclusively for the MCCCW with 43 pieces made in various colourways.
Autumn Hedgerow vase. Designed by Jeanne McDougall. Produced exclusively for the MCCCW with 32 pieces in all.
Bottle Oven vase. Designed by Beverley Wilkes. Produced exclusively for the MCCCW in a limited edition of 100.
Bougainvillea vase. Designed by Anji Davenport. Produced exclusively for the MCCCW with 42 pieces.
Clover vase. Designed by Emma Bossons. Produced exclusively for the MCCCW with 70 pieces in all in various colourways.
Frogs vase. Designed by Siân Leeper. Produced exclusively for the MCCCW with 40 pieces.
November vase. Designed by Nicola Slaney. Produced exclusively for the MCCCW with 30 pieces.
Penstemon vase. Designed by Nicola Slaney. Produced exclusively for the MCCCW with 20 pieces.
Peony jug. Designed by Philip Gibson. Produced exclusively for the MCCCW with 40 pieces.
Quayside vase. Designed by Debbie Hancock. Produced exclusively for the MCCCW with 38 pieces.
Spring Flora. Designed by Jeanne McDougall. Produced exclusively for the MCCCW with 32 pieces.
Wisdom vase. Produced exclusively for the MCCCW in a limited edition of 50.
Gentian collection. Designed by Philip Gibson. Trials on different shapes were sold at the MCCCW.
Hybrid plates. Designed by Rachel Bishop. Specifically commissioned for the Cancer BACUP award ceremony and presented to seven recipients. Each plate produced in a different colourway. An additional award of a Trout vase was given to Dr Derek Crowther as a Lifetime Achievement award.
2000
Hepaticas range. Designed by Emma Bossons.
Hellebores range. Designed by Nicola Slaney.

'Traps for the Unwary' or Fakes and Restoration

If you choose to start collecting pottery, by which I mean earthenware, stoneware, terra cotta and their related products, of which Moorcroft is a part, as opposed to a porcelain product, then restoration is something that you will inevitably come across because of the nature of the material. The fact that Moorcroft pottery is so collectable and can fetch significant prices in its field makes it worth the effort and cost of restoration. The fact that Moorcroft has now been a collectable field for just about thirty years, even more so in the last ten to fifteen years or so, means that fewer rare or sought after pieces are coming onto the market.

However, this is not something that should be off putting in anyway. If anything, it should be seen as a challenge to overcome or accept. If you want to add rare or unusual pieces to your collection, either in terms of shape or surface design, then sometimes you have to include restored pieces (if only until something similar in better condition comes along). The trick is to make sure that you are paying the right price for a restored piece and not for something that is supposed to be perfect. You won't have any problem with specialist established dealers because they are or should be more interested in cultivating a longstanding client. Where you might come across problems is with some general dealers who are not always as aware of restored pieces, sometimes offering pieces they genuinely thought were perfect. Here, of course, you as the buyer are left with the well worn phrase "buyer beware" as at the end of the day it is really up to you so train yourself to be able to spot restoration if not buying from specialist dealers or auction houses where guaranteed condition reports are available.

All commercial restoration can be spotted, no matter how good it is, all you have to do is teach yourself how to look for it and how to identify it. All the restoration you are ever likely to come across on Moorcroft is what is called 'plastic', meaning that it is made of a non-ceramic material and has not been fired. Even though the filler used to replace a chip or larger area of body can be very hard, the surface treatment used to imitate the transparent glaze, especially on Moorcroft, is where all restoration can be spotted. Ceramic wares are hard and cold (unless they are sitting on a radiator), whereas restoration is soft and will be warm or rather retain warmth after it has been held for a short period.

So how do you spot restoration? The first thing to do is to look at the piece, without picking it up, and ask yourself where the piece would be most 'likely' to be knocked. The rim, the base, the widest part, the spout, the knop, the base of the handle, the neck of a figure, any extended parts of the body, these are all likely places. You will then be able to pick up the piece and examine it more closely, using an eye glass if you wish, although after a short time of spotting damage you will soon become more confident about recognising it and put the eye glass away. The most valuable tools you can ever use to spot restoration, cracks and chips are your fingers, eyes and teeth. Personally, I avoid using a pin or coin for obvious reasons (you leave a trail of destruction if you find any restoration that won't please the vendor whether they knew the piece was restored or not), also it is sign to others that you don't really know what you are doing. For beginners of course a pin or coin used in the right way can certainly confirm your suspicions. The best way to use a pin is to lightly tap onto the surface, not drag it across, so that you can hear the differences between the high pitched hard surface of the glazed body opposed to the duller flat sound of the plastic restoration. Lightly drag your fingernails across an area you suspect might be restored and notice any changes in the freedom of movement or lack of it, across the surface of the ware. Restored/plastic areas will always have a different surface sheen or texture to that of the glass hard ceramic surface.

You should also be able to see restored areas, easier with practice of course, by the variation in colour tones or consistency of colour, as it is very, very difficult to exactly match in-glaze or even on-glaze colours that were in use thirty, forty or ninety years ago. Once you think you might have located a repaired area, you can then check for warmth and sound. As restoration is made-up of plastic materials the restored area will hold and conduct heat therefore holding your hand over a suspect area, taking it away for a moment and then returning it highlight which parts of the body went cold and those that stayed warm. As a final indicator, you can gently tap your teeth against the surface of the suspect area to hear if it makes a sharp and hard ting, for a ceramic body, or a dull thud for a restored area. It may not sound like something to recommend but if you go to a major ceramic auction in London, New York or Canada, you will probably see a few people seemingly biting into pieces of ceramics. It is very effective and it works.

All the above can only be gained through practice, so the more pieces you pick up and check the better. Even if you don't intend to buy a piece, the faster and more efficiently you can master the art of detecting restoration the better. Even if you find, by looking at pieces you already have, that you have unknowingly purchased restored items and there is little you can do about it (although do try to return such items if recently bought as the seller may not have been aware and could themselves do something about it), you can at least learn from the experience.

There is nothing whatsoever wrong with buying restored, chipped, cracked items so long as you are aware of the fact and the item is, in your view, correctly priced to reflect that fact. There are plenty of collectors who might well pay hundreds, even thousands of pounds for a damaged or restored item, if they know the rarity of the piece and assess that the price is acceptable. There are numerous reasons for collecting, such as purely for decorative effect, where damage is less of consideration than price, but I won't go into these. The reasons for what and how you collect are entirely personal, I just hope that the above might come in useful.

'Fakes' is probably the most unsavoury word when talking about the creative work of either an individual or a team of people involved in the making of an object. This word, however is nothing new to Moorcroft which, as a rather sad reflection of its success over the years, has had to put up with such imitations, fakes or copies. In the 1920s Shelley made an outright copy of the Pomegranate pattern. It took just a word from William, and production of the offending object was halted less than four weeks after it had started. Other Pomegranate fakes have been noted over the years, such was the popularity of the pattern, even a two-handled biscuit tin has been found with the design.

What is very disconcerting is the growing number of fakes of the modern designs as well as of the old and they all seem to be coming from the Far East. But there are easy ways to avoid these more recent imitations. Invariably the body is completely wrong, being both to brilliant white and even porcelaineous or certainly translucent. The painting is thin and watery in appearance as it has been applied on top of the fired body. Somewhere along the line, the imitators seem to have become confused as some of the shapes, especially those with long handles with points at the top, have been taken from a different pottery, the shapes are more like some Minton Secessionist wares. I remember seeing some fake Mamoura designs at the Frankfurt Gift fair, made in the Far East, on a stand not very far from the Moorcroft stand. These Mamoura pieces were very badly coloured and very light in weight.

Many of these fakes are often not being sold or marked as Moorcroft, they are made by manufacturers hoping to jump on a bang wagon. What is more worrying is when someone starts to make moulds from the real object and then to colour and mark them as the real thing as seems to be happening in Stoke-on-Trent with some miniature vases less than 2" high.

What you might also come across is some later decorated, to put it politely, Moorcroft wares that were sold as blanks or rejects. Inevitably, the painting will not be right, the colours will not anything like the real thing and, of course, the tube-lining will be amateur to say the least.

Moorcroft and the Internet

This is a story of both success and failure. On the one hand there is the singular failure of Moorcroft Pottery PLC or more specifically perhaps the collectors club, to make better use of the Internet to promote, educate or even publicise their own history and wares, let alone try to sell anything related to the company; books; enamels; stoneware; the collectors club; tickets to club meeting, etc. Yes, there is a www.moorcroft.com site, the only 'legal' web site as a recently added legal note proclaims but this site will shortly be four years old and very little has altered or been added since it was first launched. If you want to see some images and related text for the 1999 limited editions, special editions or tableware ranges then this is the place to go. This attitude towards the Internet is perhaps more symptomatic of a general British antipathy towards this new medium, certainly the reverse is the case in the United States where there is an enormous amount of activity with companies, clubs and societies making productive use of their home web sites. But this lack of appreciation and understanding of how other countries, perhaps less restricted in the accessibility and use of the Internet is the cause of some of the reticence of the company in ploughing ahead and creating a superb home web site. There is of course the expense to consider and perhaps there is a lack of funding for such an enterprise but just think of all those 'special' or 'limited edition' pieces Moorcroft could be offering to those who register/purchase on their on-line site. As I sit here, with the Internet having now been running constantly in the background for over four hours at a cost of 10 cents (USA) (together with a monthly charge of $19) log on charge, my mind is wondering to how easy it would be to receive an e-mail saying that my annual subscription was due and press the highlighted word 'renew' to charge my credit card, all my details having been input into my own profile page . . . Dream on. Whilst, ideally, clicking through the latest e-mailed edition of the Moorcroft club magazine I might even be tempted just to click on a 'Buy Now' button which would be a totally automated process again through my 'profile' information. It would certainly be a great deal easier and faster than the snail-mail method. Alternatively, perhaps Moorcroft pottery has a gentleman's agreement that sales and information on the making should be left to certain retailers to exploit. I am, hopefully, speaking out of turn as even as I write I expect there is a glorious new web site about to be launched.

Until that time if you are looking for a really good 'fully loaded' (comprehensive) web site with information about 'some' of the recent or current designs, good illustrations as well as information relating to the flowers used then the best web site appears to be Talents of Windsor (www.talentsofwindsor.com), probably the most prestigious UK retail outlets for new Moorcroft Pottery. I say 'some' of the recent or current designs as being retailers the owners of Talents of Windsor choose what stock they want for their shop which means that certain designs are not represented. In fact, I will go further and say that I would highly recommend reading the 'About Moorcroft', 'How it's Made', etc., this is exactly the sort of quality information, including all the latest year marks and decorators marks, one would have expected to find on the Moorcroft's own web site. There are also biographies on each of the designers not to mention a 'collectors chat' page, articles and images related to the numerous awards the pottery has achieved over the years and much, much more. This site is also 'regularly' updated. I can only wonder at the volume of business that this web site achieves from all over the world, especially when Internet searchers, from the comfort of their armchairs, must find what they might have considered to be obvious web site so woefully lacking. This web site is a definite must for anyone interested in learning about the manufacturing process and current production. For the history of the wares and lives of William and Walter Moorcroft you will have be to content with the odd article on the Internet and the numerous printed articles and books.

Another very interesting web site for today's Moorcroft is that of Garland Homes (www.garland-holmes.com). What is so interesting about this site is that they appear to have been given permission to reproduce the entire latest Moorcroft giftware and tableware catalogue on their site using the scanned images of each page of the brochure, perhaps something one might have thought the company itself might have wanted to do. In any event, this is the site where you can find 'all' of the current designs on offer and even some reproductions of pages from brochures going back to 1997, excepting some of those pieces that are made for special events.

But what of the old Moorcroft on the Internet. In 1998/99 the Internet, in particular Ebay, had plenty of very interesting Moorcroft, with many 'fresh to the market' good quality and even rare pieces being offered for sale. In 2001, far more 'new' or 'post-war' wares can now be found for sale. What web sites like Ebay are seemingly very good at is throwing up the occasional unknown or rare shape and/or pattern which is, of course, put up for sale by an unsuspecting seller. These items are usually cleaned up by the specialist Moorcroft dealers in various parts of the world who are constantly monitoring such web sites. Inevitably, there are pitfalls when buying on the Internet with sellers often totally unaware of or unskilled in being able to spot issues related of condition. There are, of course, numerous potential problems with bidding on items in an on-line auction especial on Moorcroft because of its international popularity. Over the last three years I have noticed several cases of suspect on-line sales. Good quality pieces are put up for sale and after a few days the piece has gained some interest with four or five bids and by the end of the sale the price has gone up and the piece has seemingly sold. On closer investigation by looking up the e-mail addresses of all the bidders you might be surprised to find that all or most of the addresses belong to members of the same family, one of whom has put the item up for sale. There are a few ways of finding out such information and some photo related software packages that can also help. The so-called successful bidder being careful to load 'praise' on the seller and vica versa after the sale. On one occasion, an identical situation to that above happened, where the sellers were not even in possession of the item being posted for sale as they had only just purchased the item from another on-line sale a couple of days before. This was accomplished by taking the image from the first on-line sale and re-using it on the second site. The idea being, to sell the item on, hopefully for a profit, before having to pay the bill of the first on-line sale. The word, as ever, is buyer beware.

Genuine mistakes on behalf of the ordinary unsuspecting seller on such web sites, such as not spotting a minor hairline crack, chip or even restoration, more often than not lead to a piece being welcomed back by the seller and the sale rescinded, as most genuine sellers really want to establish a cleaner than clean, honest reputation. This they achieve through extremely good feed back from pleased customers. Returning things is also a great deal easier than you might think. In countries like the United States, wrapping and sending packages is very easy, almost something of a weekly occurrence.

Just as a matter of interest it is not just the Moorcroft pottery you will find for sale on these web sites. You will also came across old Moorcroft collectors club catalogues on the Internet, which can go for between £10/£15 for old editions more than four or five years old and even £4/£5 for some of the latest editions. Books, auction catalogues and sometimes posters and other related material might also be posted on sites.

If you want to buy with impunity on the Internet you need to establish very good relationships with specialist Moorcroft dealers or auction houses. Of the major auction houses only Sotheby's have established an Internet site, www.sothebys.com, where there are frequent on-line sales that include Moorcroft items together with promotion of catalogue sales. At least with this web site anything you buy is covered by much the same conditions of business as any of the live sales. All on-line sales are subject to buyers commission and local sales tax, if you live in the United Sates. Shipping charges are added and all these are simply explained before you bid on any item. In 2001, Sothebys.com presented several on-line auctions of the Harriman Judd collection of British Art Pottery presented and promoted along with the two live sales. In each of the on-line sales there were many pieces of Moorcroft amongst the items offered. Whilst the whole sale total for these on-line sales did exceedingly well, the Moorcroft proved especially successful with several pieces drawing up to fifteen bids or more before a successful resolution. The ability to attract bidders, many of them new, from all continents across the globe without the need to subscribe to various catalogues has proved to be highly successful.

Establishing contacts with dealers on the Internet can be a very productive way for adding items to your collection, even to the point of asking dealers to look out for specific items of interest. After all, it is the dealers who are going to be spending most if the time looking in the right places when you can perhaps only spend a few hours on the occasional weekend. Relationships with dealers are often best established in person to start with either through their shop or retail outlet or at Antique fairs or Antique centres. One of the best reasons for establishing good relations in this way is that if the dealer knows exactly what you are looking for then you might well be offered the item first, before the dealer puts an item out for general sale. Such a service is something that you should also be willing to pay for in some form or other, after all, you have been saved a great deal of time, travelling expenses, etc., in the quest for such items. Such transactions are mutually beneficial but in the long run as a collector you will almost certainly benefit from the odd reduced price.

Backstamps and Other Methods of Dating

Because we are basically taking about one pottery or rather one family in terms of design out put there was little need or requirement for frequently changing the marks. It was only after Walter Moorcroft supposedly retired in 1987, although he still contributed designs in 1999, with the arrival of the new owners that a new and every changing and additionally more complex set of marks began to be introduced. At one time there where so many different marks – retailer mark, year mark, designer mark, pottery mark, tube-liner and paintresses marks, limited edition marks, etc, that there was hardly any room for the special 'signed and dated' signatures at promotional events arranged throughout the year.

During the Macintyre years there were printed marks indicating a range or style of ware, other early printed marks carried the retailers name or a combination of the retailers name with a style or range that was exclusive to that retailer. These printed marks might additionally have a hand painted script signature or monogram, with or without the 'des' for 'designed by' this combination might also appear as an incised mark. The early signatures mostly appear to have used a green colour with blue becoming a more standard colour later. On some pieces, you might also find an applied paper label added by the retailer, with a name and location, or a William Moorcroft applied paper label applied at his Cobridge pottery.

The next series of marks relate to the early years of William establishing his own pottery in Cobridge from 1913. The signature or monogram (often depending on the size of the item) were continued and were always and only executed by William himself. They are not 'facsimile' signatures but 'actual' signatures by William. In the first year of production it would appear that many of the pieces from the first firings where actually dated with the year and month together with a signature which was the only mark. Sometimes, often for a significant reason, a date and or name might be added that related to an exhibition or event that the items were destined for such as the British Industries Fair or the 1924 Wembley Exhibition. By 1914, William introduced a stamped or impressed mark of MOORCROFT over BURSLEM. This mark might also have an impressed shape number included but would usually have the painted signature or monogram. By 1916, the word ENGLAND had been added below BURSLEM and the script signature starts to appear in blue as the standard colour. In 1918, the words MADE IN were added, as with most other manufacturers with markets in America, the mark becoming MOORCROFT over MADE IN ENGLAND. This was the standard mark until 1928 following the issuing if the Royal Warrant to the pottery, the mark changing to an impressed facsimile of the 'W. Moorcroft' signature with 'Potter to HM the Queen'. There is also a new circular applied paper label complete with the Royal Lion and Unicorn emblem that has the script signature of William and 'Potter to HM The Queen'. From 1936 following the death of King George V the paper label changed to 'Potter to HM Queen Mary.'

The script signature and the monogram from about 1918 onward became more linear as demands on Williams's time become greater.

Typical early Macintyre Florian ware mark printed in brown with hand painted signature and "des." more often than not in green. 1898-1905. The printed mark sometimes occurs with the pattern registration number. Other early printed marks include Gesso Faience (introduced by Harry Barnard but still in use on early William Moorcroft wares) and Butterfly Ware.

A common early brown printed mark on Macintyre wares that was used between 1904-1913, which sometimes appears with a pattern registration number. Note the methodical W.M. and des., script monogram painted in green compared to the later hurried angular script generally found after 1913.

This is an example of a retailers printed mark, Liberty & Co, with a relatively methodical full script signature. This mark dating from between 1903-1913. During this period and during the early years of the Cobridge works numerous dated pieces can be found often with the month and year of the piece hand painted along with the painted monogram or signature. Other retailer's marks include Osler and Shreve & Son.

With the opening of the Cobridge works new marks were introduced. For the first two or three years of full production an impressed upper case MOORCROFT BURSELM was introduced, along with the hand painted monogram or script signature. Sometimes shape numbers can also be found although these marks were not frequently used. By 1916 an upper case ENGLAND was added to the impressed mark. The paper label was used by retailers to indicate a price as well as numbering pieces for exhibitions.

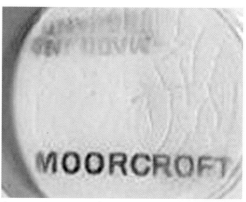

By 1918 the words "MADE IN ...." had to be included on wares imported into America and with such a strong following in America the new wording was quickly included. During the 1920s a larger, more distinct upper case MOORCROFT was introduced. This mark, with script signature in blue, became the standard mark until 1928 when the new Royal Warrant initiated another change.

Large impressed MOORCROFT in conjunction with uppercase MADE IN ENGLAND was used during the early 1950s through to 1986. This mark also occurs with Walter Moorcroft's monogram or script signature. Walter only carrying out the full script signature on important pieces and/or on special pieces.

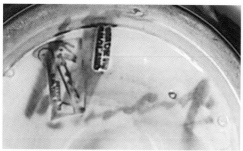

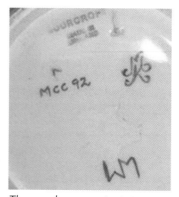

In 1928 following the awarding of the Royal Warrant, William started to use an impressed stamp with a facsimile signature together with the words "Potter to HM The Queen" used until 1949. At this time a paper label was also introduced with the same wording which was in use until 1953. In 1936, the wording changed to "Potter to HM Queen Mary" following the death of King George V. Here you can also see the full script signature of William.

The marks now start to get more complex. There is still the basic uppercase MOORCROFT and MADE IN ENGLAND to which a WM monogram has been added for William John Moorcroft. John Moorcroft painted his full signature, J. Moorcroft, on some of the larger or prestige pieces. A year cipher has been added, the candle indicating 1992, as well as decorators marks. On this mark there is also the mark of the Moorcroft Collectors Club indicating pieces that were designed for and sold to members only.

This is much the same as the previous mark but with the addition of a painted 'C' within a circle denoting copyright. Until a stamp was introduced this mark was hand painted. The mark being introduced in an effort to dissuade copyists from reproducing the designs.

This shows the full script signature painted by John Moorcroft which appears on only large pieces, exhibition pieces or special pieces.

No great changes in the marks took place until the arrival of Walter in 1947 and even then, except for an alteration in the painted script signature, there was little immediate need to alter the mark. Walter did, of course, use the same monogram WM but his initials were more angular and straight. Another way to notice the difference is that Walter used a more slate/blue colouring than his father William and this continued for a number of years. Only later did Walters' signature and/or monogram appear in brown and/or green usually depending on the palette being used on the item.

From 1953 to 1978 Walter gained the Royal Warrant and used an applied paper label with the words 'By Appointment Potter to the late Queen Mary.' During this period the word MOORCROFT become bolder. Unlike his father, Walter did not see the necessity nor have the time to paint his signature or monogram onto every piece of ware produced. The vast majority of production pieces were painted with Walters's initials by one of the paintresses. On many occasions Walter did sign significant pieces or limited editions.

Things seem to have carried on in much the same vein during the two year period when the Churchill Group run by the Roper brothers' owned the Moorcroft Pottery. It was not until 1987 following the take over of the pottery by Hugh Edwards and Richard Dennis together with their respective partners, that a new order emerged along with a requisite new look. Sally Tuffin took over as the chief designer with Walter now acting as consultant. The mark therefore changed to reflect the fact that Walter's brother John was now on the board of directors continuing the family tradition. A new square WM monogram was developed which was impressed on most of the production pots. John Moorcroft signed the larger more prestigious pieces with a full script signature.

It was also during these early years that idea of including the actual designers monogram along with the paintresses and tube-liners monogram and/or symbol was developed. S.T. DES for Sally Tuffin began to be included. Year symbols then followed in 1990 with the introduction of an impressed arrow followed by a bell in 1991, a candlestick in 1992, a diamond form in 1993, an eye for 1994, a flag in 1995, a gate in 1996, a HC monogram for the Centenary year, an iron for 1998, a jug/pitcher for 1999 and a key with a double 'M' for the teeth for 2000.

For a full set of painters' and tube-liners' marks see the two book by Hugh Edwards, these also have numerous retailers and special marks used during the last ten years or so.

Whilst we are talking about the base of Moorcroft pots in recent years it is certainly worth mentioning one very important mark that has been causing problems, namely the 'silver slither' second mark.

Moorcroft pots have to reach a very high standard to pass the eagle eyes of the quality controller. You would be amassed at the minute detail the likes of you and I would have to look at a 'less than perfect' specimen to see anything vaguely wrong with it. Minor bits of tube-lining might have come free from the body; a minor air bubble bursts through the glaze on firing; a speck of dust or powder causes a blemish or indeed a layer of colouring might inadvertently have been forgotten. Whatever the fault the pieces are quickly spotted by highly trained eyes and placed on the seconds shelf. Here the pieces are all given a permanent deep gauge through the WM monogram with a steel that leaves a thin silver slither through the mark. These 'almost' perfect pieces are only sold in the factory shop.

The trouble starts when some people start buying seconds and grind out the sliver lines and sell them as perfect. There will always be a tell-tail depression if you look very hard but the point is you shouldn't have to look very hard. If in doubt, run your finger across the WM monogram and try to feel any sudden depression. It's just another thing to get used to doing, just as looking for restoration, before committing to buying a piece.

The Moorcroft Collector's Cub

Founded in 1987, with Gill Moorcroft as the club secretary, the collector's club has now become a large international club with a significant role to play in the fortunes of the company. As I have already mentioned, one area that would seem ideally suited to augment the effectiveness and ease of communication of the collectors club is the Internet, more specifically through their own W. Moorcroft Plc. web site. Alas, this aspect of the collectors club has yet to come to fruition, although I feel sure it will do in the near future.

For now the practical aspects of membership means that you will get four Newsletter Magazines packed with insider info on the latest comings and goings at the factory and not just about Moorcroft pottery but also about Moorcroft enamels. The magazine has been getting fatter and fatter in the last few years; the latest edition was up to 64 pages, as a consequence what used to be three editions a year was increased to four at the end of 2001. The subscription fee also went up, of course, to adjust for this. The newsletter is now very much designed as a vehicle for member's comments and questions, with past and forthcoming membership events reported at length. The promotion of specials, limited editions and special events such as visits by certain designers, or board members where pieces will be additionally signed and dated are an essential. Certain retailers, of course, have also taken to commissioning a special piece of their own with their own special mark that are only for sale from that retailer. Articles are largely about current designs, alterations and developments to the works, about recent discontinued lines. The family aspect of magazine is developed through the up-to-date new arrivals to Moorcroft employees, as well as personal profiles of designers and other workers. Private interests, achievements, and pursuits of employees such as marathon running, rock climbing and visits to foreign lands are all dutifully reported.

Being a member enables you to get discounts, advance notification of certain events and the ability to book tickets to membership only collector's day events and/or special dinner events. There are annual collector's club only pieces along with member's day event pieces and now there are exclusive special pieces only available to certain members depending on the number of years you have been a member, this is called the Star Membership. You get the full 5 stars after 15 years of membership, 4 stars after 12 years and 3 stars after 9 years, etc. Just by being a member the number of pieces only you can buy as a member, often limited to one piece per family or membership, in one year not to mention the number of limited edition pieces and/or numbered pieces and you could have a fair number of pieces without buying any of the ordinary ranges offered to the general public.

The big event of the year is the Open day or weekend as it become as it has spread over two days and sometimes three. Held in May or June the amount of events on offer has to be seen to be believed. The day starts with a lecture usually by a popular television personality related to antiques, a behind the scenes wonder around the factory followed by the all important auction of one-off trail and experimental pieces, as well as pieces designed and made by the painters/ess and tube-liners. The factory shop is, of course, open as is the museum. A 10% discount is available for members from the factory shop as per usual.

Factory tours, which last about an hour, are on Mondays, Wednesdays and Thursdays at 11.00am and 2.00pm and Fridays at 11.00am only.

The Museum and Shop opening hours are Monday-Friday 10.00am-5.00pm, Saturday 9.30am-4.30pm (Closed Christmas to New Year.)

For further information contact or e-mail Elise Adams, the collectors club secretary, elisea@mooorcroft.co.uk

W.Moorcroft PLC. Sandbach Road, Burslem, Stoke-on-Trent. ST6 2DQ. England.

Telephone +44 (0) 1782 820500. Facsimile +44 (0) 1782 820501

The current membership rates are: United Kingdom & Rest of the World – £17.50. Taiwan – NT$800.00. Australia – $45.00. New Zealand – $45.00.

Bibliography

Moorcroft – A Guide to Moorcroft Pottery 1897-1993 Paul Atterbury with additional material by Beatrice Moorcroft. 1993.
Walter Moorcroft – Memories of Life and Living Walter Moorcroft. 1999.
Moorcroft – The Phoenix Years Fraser Street. 1997.
Moorcroft – Winds of Change Fraser Street. 2000.
Ceramics Francis Hannah. 1986.
Ceramics of the 1950s Graham McLaren. 1997.

Periodicals, Catalogues, etc.
Moorcroft Exhibition catalogue. Richard Dennis. 1972.
Pottery Gazette and Glass Trades Review.
Pottery and Glass Record.
The Studio.
Moorcroft Collectors Club newsletters.
Moorcroft retail brochures.
Sotheby's auction catalogues. London, Sussex and Chester.
Phillips auction catalogues.
Christies auction catalogues.
The Sentinel Newspaper.
Companies House records.
Unpublished memories of Harry Barnard.